THE EVERLASTING RIGHTEOUSNESS

THE EVERLASTING RIGHTEOUSNESS

or

How Shall Man Be Just with God?

Horatius Bonar

The Trinity Foundation
Hobbs, New Mexico

First published 1874
Revised edition copyright 1994 John W. Robbins
Published by The Trinity Foundation
Post Office Box 1666
Hobbs, New Mexico 88240
ISBN: 0-940931-41-9

"We are justified by faith. Being justified, all our sins are covered. God beholdeth us in the righteousness which is imputed, and not in the sins which we have committed. But imputation of righteousness hath covered the sins of every soul which believeth. God, by pardoning our sin, hath taken it away; so that now, although our transgressions be multiplied above the hairs of our head, yet, being justified, we are as free and as clear as if there were no one spot or stain of any uncleanness in us. Now, sin being taken away, we are made the righteousness of God in Christ. No man is blessed but in the righteousness of God: every man whose sin is taken away is blessed; therefore every man whose sin is covered is made the righteousness of God in Christ. This righteousness doth make us to appear most holy, most pure, most unblameable before him."

—Richard Hooker
on Jude

"God made him to be sin for us who knew no sin, that we might be made the righteousness of God in him. Such are we in the sight of God the Father as is the very Son of God himself. Let it be counted folly or frenzy or fury whatsoever, it is our comfort and our wisdom: we care for no knowledge in the world but this, that man hath sinned, and God hath suffered; that God hath made himself the sin of man, and that men are made the righteousness of God.

—Richard Hooker
On Justification

CONTENTS

FOREWORD

It has been nearly 2,000 years since the apostle Paul wrote his letters explaining the Gospel of justification by faith alone to the churches in Asia and Europe, and the light of the Gospel shone brilliantly in the spiritual, intellectual, and moral darkness of ancient Rome. But Antichrist, already at work in the first century, soon sat in the temple of God, expelling and persecuting the saints and suppressing the Gospel of Christ for a millennium. His dominion ended when God raised another witness to his truth in the sixteenth century.

It has been nearly 500 years since Martin Luther recovered the Gospel in Europe. Once again, in the sixteenth century, the light of justification by faith alone dispelled the spiritual, intellectual, and moral darkness of medieval Rome. The resulting civilization owed its salient features to the Gospel of Jesus Christ—to the first Christians and the Reformers—but for the past century the proclamation of that Gospel—and civilization—has been waning.

Now, nearly every day brings news of some new Roman resurgence; Antichrist is again in the ascendancy. Churches, once heirs of the Reformation, reach detente with Rome. The Roman church-state, ruled by the most absolute monarch on Earth—a monarch who claims to speak for God himself—maintains diplomatic relations with most nations on the planet. Protestants have forgotten what their forefathers protested and the truths for which they were murdered by Rome. Charismatics and evangelicals eagerly embrace the theology of Rome. The Roman religion is on the march again.

How has this happened? How did the heirs of the Reformation lose the Gospel?

Deception is the chief work of the devil, for we are told that he is a liar and the father of lies. Christ said that the devil appears as an angel of light, as a good shepherd and protector of the sheep.

The puerile portrayals of the devil on television and in the movies lead many to suppose that he is easily recognizable, but they have been easily fooled. Millions have been deceived by his false gospels, all of which replace the Gospel—the life, death, and everlasting righteousness of Jesus Christ—with something else. Those false gospels are usually not irreligious—atheism has its place in the devil's tool kit, but religion is far more useful. The road to Hell is paved with religious beliefs and observances.

The common core of the false gospels of this age is a focus on self, not Christ. Long before psychology became fashionable in the churches, they taught self-absorption. Anthropology replaced theology a century ago. Instead of proclaiming the Gospel—the good news of what Christ did for his people 2,000 years ago—they proclaimed the false gospel of what God can do for you now. Rome, of course, has taught this false gospel for centuries, saying that what makes a man acceptable to God is God's grace in his heart. That grace is received through the sacraments of the church, especially baptism and mass, and there is no salvation outside the Roman church.

But grace is not something infused—like pie filling—into human hearts. It is an attribute of God, not of man—God's unmerited favor toward his people. What makes a man acceptable to God is not God's grace in his heart, but the perfect life and obedient and substitutionary death of Jesus Christ, who fulfilled the law of God perfectly on behalf of his people. This false gospel—that we are saved by something inside us, even if it is something of allegedly divine origin—replaced the true Gospel—that we are saved only by the perfect life and death of Christ—centuries ago in the Roman church, and it is now widely accepted in most other churches. Sometimes the false gospel takes the form of the gospel of the new birth—as though being born again makes one acceptable to God—or the baptism of the Spirit, or our own good works, which give evidence of the grace of God in our hearts. Sometimes the false gospel takes the form of preaching that says that belief of the Gospel is not enough, that we must "surrender," that we must "trust," that we must "make Jesus Lord of our life," that we must "put Jesus on the throne of our life."

But the Gospel declares that we are not justified by any psychological exercises, by any infused goodness, by any feelings, intentions, or works, but simply by believing the account of Christ's life and death in the Bible. We are saved by assenting to the truth of the everlasting righteousness of Christ and acknowledging our own hopeless sinfulness.

Before Martin Luther recovered the Gospel of justification by faith alone, he was the most religious of monks. He performed all that was required of him—prayers, fastings, masses, flagellations— and more, for he was seeking evidence of the grace of God in his heart; he was surrendering totally to God. Yet Luther despaired because he saw that all his righteousnesses were as filthy rags before God. Then the light of the Gospel dawned on him, and he realized that he could not be saved by his own good feelings and good intentions, even if those good feelings and good intentions came from God, but only by an alien righteousness—the righteousness of God himself. False gospels cause men to look inside themselves, if not at their own strengths, then for evidence of what God is doing in their lives. The true Gospel is about what Jesus Christ did 2,000 years ago. It focuses our minds on him and his righteousness, not on ourselves.

Because false gospels cause men to look inward rather than outward and upward to Christ, they have taken many different forms: the false gospel of the new birth, the false gospel of the changed life, the false gospel of self-esteem, the false gospel of full surrender, the false gospel of Spirit baptism, the false gospel of grace in the heart, the false gospel of an integrated personality, the false gospel of good works, the false gospel of good intentions, the false gospel of positive thinking, the false gospel of speaking in tongues, the false gospel of letting Jesus into your heart, the false gospel of a personal relationship (or encounter or experience) with Jesus, the false gospel of following Jesus as a moral example, the false gospel of prosperity and fulfillment. The variety of subjective gospels is endless, but there is only one true Gospel, the everlasting righteousness of Christ.

This book, written by a Scottish Presbyterian minster over a century ago, is one of the best books on the Gospel ever written. It is clear, simple, and thorough in its explanation of justification through faith alone. Horatius Bonar (1808–1889) was also a poet and hymn-writer, and one of his best known hymns is "Not What My Hands Have Done." Here are the words in which he there expressed the Gospel:

Not what my hands have done
Can save my guilty soul.
Not what my toiling flesh has borne
Can make my spirit whole.
Not what I feel or do
Can give me peace with God.
Not all my prayers and sighs and tears
Can bear my awful load.

Thy work alone, O Christ,
Can ease this weight of sin.
They blood alone, O Lamb of God,
Can give me peace within.
Thy love to me, O God,
Not mine, O Lord, to Thee
Can rid me of this dark unrest
And set my spirit free.

Thy grace alone, O God,
To me can pardon speak.
Thy power alone, O Son of God,
Can this sore bondage break.
No other work, save thine,
No other blood will do.
No strength save that which is divine
Can bear me safely through.

I bless the Christ of God;
I rest on love divine.
And with unfaltering lip and heart,
I call this Savior mine.
His cross dispels each doubt;
I bury in his tomb

Each thought of unbelief and fear,
Each lingering shade of gloom.

I praise the God of grace;
I trust his truth and might.
He calls me his; I call him mine—
My God, my joy, my light.
'Tis he who saveth me, and freely pardon gives;
I love because he loveth me
I live because he lives.

John W. Robbins
June 1994

PREFACE

The awakened conscience of the sixteenth century betook itself to "the righteousness of God."

There it found refuge, at once from condemnation and from impurity.

Only by "righteousness" could it be pacified, and nothing less than that which is divine could meet the case.

At the cross this "righteousness" was found; human, yet divine: provided for man and presented to him by God for relief of conscience and justification of life. On the one word τετέλεσται, "It is finished," as on a heavenly resting place, weary souls sat down and were refreshed. The voice from the tree did not summon them to *do*, but to be satisfied with what was *done*. Millions of bruised consciences there found healing and peace.

Belief in that finished work brought the sinner into favor with God, and it did not leave him in uncertainty as to this. The justifying work of Calvary was God's way, not only of bringing pardon, but of securing certainty. It was the only perfect thing which had ever been presented to God in man's behalf; and so extraordinary was this perfection that it might be used by man in his transactions with God as if it were his own.

The knowledge of this sure justification was life from the dead to multitudes. All over Europe, from the Apennines to the Grampians, from the Pyrenees to the Carpathians, went the glad tidings that man is justified freely, and that God wishes him to know that he is justified. It was not merely a new thought for man's intellect, but a new discovery for his soul (1) as to the true source of spiritual health, namely, the setting of a man's *conscience* right with God; and (2) as to the continuation of that health, namely, the keeping of the *conscience* right.

The fruit of this was not merely a healthy personal religion, but a renovated intellect and a noble literature, and, above all, a pure worship. It was an era of resurrection. The graves were opened, and the congregation of the dead became the Church of the living. Christendom awoke and arose. The resurrection dew fell far and wide, and it has not yet ceased to fall.

For ages, Christianity had grovelled in the dust, smothered with semi-pagan rites, ready to die—if not already dead—bound hand and foot by a semi-idolatrous priesthood; unable to do aught for a world which it had been sent to regenerate. Now, "it was lifted up from the Earth, and made to stand upon its feet as a man, and a man's heart was given to it."

A new *conscience* was born, and with a new conscience came new life and power. Nothing had been seen like this since the age of the apostles.

The doctrine of another's righteousness reckoned to us for justification before God is one of the links that knit together the first and the sixteenth centuries, the Apostles and the Reformers. The creeds of the Reformation overleap fifteen centuries and land us at once in the Epistle to the Romans. Judicial and moral cleansing was what man needed. In that epistle we have both the imputed and imparted righteousness—not the one without the other; both together, and inseparable, but each in its own order, the former the root or foundation of the latter.

It was not Martin Luther merely who took up the old watchword, "The just shall live by faith," and thus found the answer of a good conscience toward God. To thousands of hearts it came like a voice from Heaven, they knew not how. Sunshine from above had fallen upon one grand text, the text which the age needed. Men recognized the truth thus supernaturally lighted up. "The nations came to its light, and kings to the brightness of its rising." The inquiring men of that age, though not borrowing from each other, betook themselves to this truth and text. From every kingdom of Europe came the same voice, and every Protestant Confession bore witness to the unanimity of awakened Christendom. The long-needed, long-missing truth had been found; and ευρηκα [*Eureka!*] was the cry of gladness announcing the discovery.

Our fathers saw that this truth was the basis of all real spiritual life. That which was superficial, and morbid, and puny, and second-rate, might do with some less deep, less broad foundation; but all that is healthy, and noble and daring and happy and successful in religion must rest here: "The just shall live by faith."

Religion is fashionable in our age. But is it that which sprang up, after centuries of darkness, among our fathers in Europe? Is it that of the apostles and prophets? Is it the calm yet thorough religion which did such great deeds in other days? Has it gone deep into the conscience? Has it filled the heart? Has it pervaded the man? Or has it left the conscience unpacified, the heart unfilled, the man unchanged, save with some external appliances of religiousness which leave him *hollow* as before? There is at this moment many an aching spirit, bitterly conscious of this hollowness. Merely understanding the doctrine, the profession, the good report of others, the bustle of work will not fill the soul. God himself must be there with his covering righteousness, his cleansing blood, his quickening Spirit. Without this, religion is but a shell; holy services are dull and irksome. Joy in God, which is the soul and essence of worship, is unknown. Sacraments, prayer meetings, religious services, labors of charity and will not make up for the living God.

How much of *unreality* there may be in the religious life of our age, it is for each individual to determine for himself that he may not be deceived nor lose his reward.* All unreality is weakness as

---

*One who knows the "religious world" well, and passed through its hollowness, thus writes: "It is just two years since he came in a way as certainly miraculous as ever he spake with a voice to Paul or any other, and ran his plough through my heart, breaking up and tearing into shreds my old "Christian" and "professor" life, showing me *death,* death amidst all, and leading me, though with terrible struggles and opposition from the old heart and its pride, into something like a knowledge of himself, the living personal Jesus; though, alas, how feeble, how dark, how slow, has been the progress! Before that, I was in a condition in which I verily believe (though it may seem unkind and morbid to say so) the great part of the professing church is at the present day, ministers as well as people. I know the kind of intercourse I had with many who pass for as good Christians as are to be found; and I know this, that very many who could talk hotly about doctrine, who would laugh and make merry, smile at my foolish jesting, showed no inclination whatever to join in speaking of the personal living Lord himself, after he came by his strong arm of power, and made me wish more to speak of him. I think it is well that you should be told such things. Cry aloud, spare not; show to the house of Israel their sins. There is far too much assuming even on the part of the faithful ones, that many of

well as irksomeness; the sooner that we are stripped of unreality the better, both for peace and for usefulness.

Men with their feet firmly set on Luther's rock, "the righteousness of God," filled with the Spirit, and pervaded with the peace of God do the great things in the church; others do the little.

The men of robust spiritual health are they who, like Luther, have made sure of their filial relationship to God. They shrink from no battle nor succumb to any toil. The men who go to work with an unascertained relationship give way in the warfare and faint under the labor: their life is not perhaps a failure or defeat, but it is not a victory; it is not a triumph.

"We do not war after the flesh" (2 Corinthians 10:3), and "our weapons are not carnal" (2 Corinthians 10:4). Our battle is not fought in the way that the old man would have us to fight it. It is "the fight of *faith*" (1 Timothy 6:12). It is not by *doubting* but by *believing* that we are saved; it is not by *doubting* but by *believing* that we overcome. Faith leads us first of all to Abel's "more excellent sacrifice" (Hebrews 11:4). By faith we quit Ur and Egypt and Babylon, setting our face to the eternal city (Hebrews 11:16). By faith we offer up our Isaacs, and worship "leaning on the top of our staff," and "give commandment concerning our bones." By faith we choose affliction with the people of God and despise Egypt's

---

their flock are only *in a low state,* and that the mere calling them to go out of the world is enough. No. While there may be an isolated case of this sort, I believe that where worldliness and inconsistency are so widespread as they are, where so many are known only by profession, and by no other single mark or fruit of the Lord's people, it tells of something worse. The ploughshare must be sent deeper. It must bring up earth which has not yet been searched. A great number are awakened and interested in youth, who by and by find a sort of peace, through some kind of wrong preaching or daubing with untempered mortar, along with the blindness of their own heart. Such peace is not founded on *personal contact with the living One;* and when business, or advancing years, or worldly entanglements come in, their vessel will not hold. What have they to fall back upon? They do not like to abandon their profession; nay, there hangs about them a sort of spurious and galvanic life, which blinds them. But they know not the Lord of life. The good Lord help you to deal with such souls; and may he anoint you afresh, and give you his own wisdom and discernment to speak so as to draw souls, and call them to new life in the Lord."

treasures. By faith we keep our passover, pass through the Red Sea, overthrow Jerichos, subdue kingdoms, work righteousness, stop the mouths of lions, quench the violence of fire, turn to flight the armies of the aliens, and refuse deliverance in the day of trial, that we may obtain a better resurrection (Hebrews 11:35).

It is "believing" from first to last. We begin, we go on, we end in *faith*. The faith that *justifies* is the faith that *overcomes* (1 John 5:4). By faith we obtain the "good report" both with God and man. By faith we receive forgiveness; by faith we live; by faith we work, and endure, and suffer; by faith we win the crown—a crown of righteousness which shall be ours in the day of the appearing of him who is *our righteousness*.

The Grange, Edinburgh
November 1872

How Shall Man Be Just with God?

1

God's Answer to Man's Question

How may I, a sinner, draw near to him in whom there is no sin, and look upon his face in peace?

This is the great question which, at some time or other, every one of us has asked. This is one of the awful problems which man in all ages has been attempting to solve. There is no evading it; he must face it.

That man's answers to this question should have been altogether wide of the mark is only what might have been expected. He does not really understand the import of the question which he, with much earnestness perhaps, is putting, nor discern the malignant character of that evil which he yet feels to be a barrier between him and God.

That man's many elaborate solutions to the problem which has perplexed the race since evil entered should have been unsatisfactory, is not surprising, seeing his ideas of human guilt are so superficial, his thoughts of himself so high; his views of God so low.

But that, when God has interposed as an interpreter to answer the question and to solve the problem, man should be so slow to accept the divine solution as given in the word of God, betrays an amount of unteachableness and self-will which it is difficult to comprehend. The preference which man has always shown for his own theories upon this point is unaccountable, save upon the supposition that he has but a poor discernment of the evil forces with which he professes to battle; a faint knowledge of the spiritual havoc which has been wrought in himself; a very vague perception of what law and righteousness are; a sorrowful ignorance of that Divine Being with whom, as lawgiver and judge, he knows that he has to do; and a low appreciation of eternal holiness and truth.

Man has always treated sin as a misfortune, not a crime; as disease, not as guilt; as a case for the physician, not for the judge. Herein lies the essential faultiness of all mere human religions or theologies. They fail to acknowledge the judicial aspect of the question as that on which the answer must hinge and to recognize the guilt or criminality of the evil-doer as that which must first be dealt with before any other answer, or approximation to an answer, can be given.

God is a Father, but he is no less a judge. Shall the judge give way to the Father, or the Father give way to the judge?

God loves the sinner, but he hates the sin. Shall he sink his love to the sinner in his hatred of the sin, or his hatred of the sin in his love to the sinner?

God has sworn that he has no pleasure in the death of the sinner (Ezekiel 18:23–32). Which of the two oaths shall be kept? Shall the one give way to the other? Can both be kept inviolate? Can a contradiction, apparently so directly, be reconciled? Which is the more unchangeable and irreversible, the vow of pity or the oath of justice?

Law and love must be *reconciled,* else the great question as to a sinner's relationship to the Holy One must remain unanswered. The one cannot give way to the other. Both must stand, else the pillars of the universe will be shaken.

The reconciliation man has often tried, for he has always had a glimpse of the difficulty. But he has failed, for his endeavors have always been in the direction of making law succumb to love.

The reconciliation God has accomplished, and, in the accomplishment, both law and love have triumphed. The one has not given way to the other. Each has kept its ground. Each has come from the conflict honored and glorified. Never has there been love like this love of God—so large, so lofty, so intense, so self-sacrificing. Never has law been seen so pure, so broad, so glorious, so inexorable.

There has been no *compromise.* Law and love have both had their full scope. Not one jot or tittle has been surrendered by either. They have both been satisfied to the full—the one in all its severity, the other in all its tenderness. Love has never been more truly love, and law has never been more truly law, than in this conjunction of the two. It has been reconciliation without compromise. God's honor has been maintained, yet man's interests have not been sacrificed.

God has done it all, and he has done it effectually and irreversibly.

Man could not have done it, even though he might have devised it. But truly he could do neither. God only could have devised and done it.

He has done it by moving the whole case into his own courts of law that it might be settled there on a righteous basis. Man could not have gone into court with the case save in the certainty that he would lose it. God comes into court, bringing man and man's whole case along with him, that upon righteous principles and in a legal way the case may be settled, at once in favor of man and in favor of God. It is this *judicial* settlement of the case that is God's one and final answer to man's long unanswered question, "How shall man be just with God?" "Wherewith shall I come before the Lord, and bow myself before the high God?" (Micah 6:6).

God provides the *basis* of the reconciliation—a basis which demonstrates that there is no *compromise* between law and love, but the full expression of both; a basis which establishes both the authority and the paternity of Jehovah, as lawgiver and Father; a basis which reveals in infinite awfulness the exceeding sinfulness of sin, the spotless purity of the statute, and the unbending character of God's governmental ordinances; a basis which yet secures, in and by law, the righteous overflow of his boundless love to the lost sons of Adam.

This basis of reconciliation between law and love God has himself not only provided, but brought into his own courts of law, proposing to the sinner that all the questions between himself and the sinner should be settled on this basis—so equitable, so friendly, so secure; and settled in judicial form, by a legal process, in which verdict is given in favor of the accused and he is clean absolved—"justified from all things."

The consent of parties to the acceptance of this basis is required in court. The law consents; the lawgiver consents; Father, Son, and Spirit consent; and *man*, the chief party interested, is asked for *his* consent. If he consents, the whole matter is settled. The verdict is issued in his favor, and henceforth he can triumph and say, "It is God that justifies; who is he that condemns?"

Sin is too great an evil for man to meddle with. His attempts to remove it do but increase it, and his endeavors to approach God in spite of it aggravate his guilt. Only God can deal with sin, either as a disease or as a crime; as a dishonor to himself, or as a hinderer of man's approach to himself. He deals with it not in some arbitrary or summary way, by a mere exercise of will or power, but by bringing it for adjudication into his own courts of law. As judge, seated in his tribunal, he settles the case, and settles it in favor of the sinner—of any sinner on Earth who will consent to the basis which he proposes. Into this court each one may freely come, on the footing of a sinner needing the settlement of the great question between him and God. That settlement is no matter of uncertainty or difficulty; it will at once be granted to each applicant. The guilty man with his case, however bad, thus legally settled, retires from court with his burden removed and his fears dispelled. He is assured that he can never again be summoned to answer for his guilt. It is righteousness that has reconciled God to him, and him to God.

As sin is too great an evil for any but God to deal with, so is righteousness too high for man to reach, too high for any but God to bring down and place at our disposal. God has brought down, and brought nigh, the righteousness. Thus the guilt which we have contracted is met by the righteousness which God has provided. The *exclusion* from the divine fellowship, which the guilt produced, is more than reversed by the new *introduction* which the righteousness places at our disposal.

May I then draw near to God and not die? May I draw near and live? May I come to him who hates sin, and yet find that the sin which he hates is no barrier to my coming, no reason for my being shut out from his presence as an unclean thing? May I renew my lost fellowship with him who made me, and made me for himself? May I worship in his holy place with safety to myself and without dishonor to him?

These are the questions with which God has dealt—and dealt with so as to ensure a blessed answer to them all—an answer which will satisfy our own troubled consciences as well as the holy law of God. His answer is *final*, and it is *effectual*. He will give no other, nor will he deal with these questions in any other way than he has done. He has introduced them into his courts of law that there they may be finally settled, and out of these courts into which God has taken them, who can withdraw them? Or what end would be served by such a withdrawal on our part? Would it make the settlement more easy, more pleasant, more sure? It would not. It would augment the uncertainty and make the perplexity absolutely hopeless.

Yet the tendency of modern thought and modern theology is to refuse the *judicial* settlement of these questions and to withdraw them from the courts into which God has introduced them. An extrajudicial adjustment is attempted, man declining to admit such a guilt as would bring him within the grasp of law and refusing to acknowledge sin to be of such a nature as to require a criminal process in solemn court, yet admitting the necessity or desirableness of the removal of the sore evil under which humanity is felt to be laboring and under which, if unremoved, it must ere long dissolve.

The history of six thousand years of evil has been lost on man. He refuses to read its awful lesson regarding sin and God's displeasure against the sinner, which that history records. The flood of evil that has issued forth from one single sin he has forgotten. The death, the darkness, the sorrow, the sickness, the tears, the weariness, the madness, the confusion, the bloodshed, the furious hatred between man and man, making Earth a suburb of Hell—all this is overlooked or misread. Man repels the thought that sin is crime which God hates with an infinite hate and which he, in his righteousness, must condemn and avenge.

If sin is such a surface thing, such a trifle as men deem it, what is the significance of this long sad story? Do earth's ten thousand graveyards, where human love lies buried, tell no darker tale? Do the millions upon millions of broken hearts and heavy eyes say that sin is but a trifle? Do the moaning of the hospital or the carnage of the battlefield, the blood-stained sword, and the death-dealing artillery proclaim that sin is a mere casualty and the human heart the seat of goodness after all? Do the earthquake, the volcano, the hurricane, the tempest speak nothing of sin's desperate evil? Do not man's aching head, and empty heart, and burdened spirit, and shaded brow, and weary brain, and tottering limbs utter—in a voice articulate beyond mistake—that sin is *guilt*? And do they not utter that guilt must be punished—punished by the Judge of all—not as a mere "violation of natural laws," but as a breach of the eternal law, which admits of no reversal: "The soul that sins, it shall die?" For without law, sin is nothing. "The strength of sin is the law" (1 Corinthians 15:56), and he who makes light of sin must defend moral confusion and injustice. He who refuses to recognize sin as *guilt* must dissolve the law of the universe or ascribe imbecility and injustice to the Judge of all.

The world has grown old in sin. It has now more than ever begun to trifle with it, either as a necessity which cannot be cured, or a partial aberration from good order which will rectify itself ere long. It is this tampering with evil, this refusal to see sin as God sees it, as the law declares it, and as the story of our race has revealed it, that has in all ages been the root of error and of wide departure from the faith once delivered to the saints. Admit the evil of sin with all its eternal consequences, and you are shut up to a divine way of dealing with it. Deny the evil of sin and the future results of that evil, and you may deny the whole revelation of God, set aside the cross, and abrogate the law.

"By the law is the knowledge of sin." Therefore the connection between sin and law must be maintained both in condemnation and in pardon. God's interposition in behalf of man must be a confirmation (not a relaxation) of law: For law cannot change, even as God cannot change nor deny himself.

Favor to the sinner must be also favor to the law. Favor to the sinner which would simply establish law or leave its sanctities untouched would be much. But favor to him which would deepen its foundations and render it more venerable, more awful than before, is unspeakably higher and surer. Even so has it been. Law has not suffered at the hands of love, nor love been cramped and frozen by law. Both have had full scope, fuller scope than if man had never fallen.

I know that love is not law, and that law is not love. In law, properly, no love inheres. It is like the balance which knows not whether it be gold or iron that is laid upon it. Yet in that combination of the judicial and the paternal, which God's way of salvation exhibits, law has become the source and vehicle of love; and love law's upholder and honorer, so that even in this sense and aspect, "love is the fulfilling of the law."*

---

*"Of law there can be no less acknowledged than that her seat is the bosom of God, her voice the harmony of the world; all things in heaven do her homage, the very least as feeling her care, and the greatest as not exempted from her power; both angels and men, and creatures of what condition soever, though

The law that was against the sinner has come to be upon the sinner's side. It is now ready to take his part in the great controversy between him and God, provided he will conduct his case on the new principles which God has introduced for the settlement of all variances between himself and the sinner; or rather, provided he will put that case into the hands of the Divine Advocate, who alone knows how to conduct it aright and to bring it to a successful issue—who is both "propitiation" and "Advocate"—the "propitiation for our sins" (1 John 2:2), "the Advocate with the Father, Jesus Christ the righteous" (1 John 2:1).

---

each in different sort and manner, yet all, with uniform consent, admiring her as the mother of their peace and joy."—Richard Hooker, *The Laws of Ecclesiastical Polity,* Book i, section 16.

2

GOD'S RECOGNITION OF SUBSTITUTION

The mere bringing the question into the courts of law would have availed nothing had there not been provision made for so ordering their processes and judgments that the sinner might be righteously *acquitted;* that God might be "just and the justifier" (Romans 3:26), "a just God and a Savior" (Isaiah 45:21); that law might be brought to be upon the sinner's side: his absolver and not his condemner.

This provision has been made by means of *substitution,* transference of the penalty from him who had incurred it to one who had not.

In human courts no such provision can be allowed, save in regard to the payment of debt. In that case, there is no difficulty as to the exchange of person and of property. If the creditor receives his money from a third party, he is satisfied, and the law is satisfied, though the debtor himself has not paid one farthing. To a certain extent, this is substitution. The idea of such a thing, therefore, is not unknown in common life and the principle of it not unacknowledged by human law.

But beyond this the law of man does not go. Substitution in any wider aspect is something about which man has never attempted to legislate. Stripe for stripe is *human* law; "by his stripes we are healed" is *superhuman,* the result of a legislation as gracious as it is divine.

Substitution is not for man to deal with: Its principle he but imperfectly understands; its details he cannot reach. They are far too intricate, too far-reaching, and too mysterious for him to grasp, or, having grasped, to found any system of legislation upon them. In this, even though willing, he must ever be helpless.

But God has affirmed *substitution* as the principle on which he means to deal with fallen man. The arrangements of his holy tribu-

8

nal, his righteous governmental processes, are such as to bring this effectually and continually into play. It is through substitution that his righteous government displays its perfection in all its transactions with the sinner.

God has introduced the principle of substitution into his courts. There he sits as judge, "just and justifying," acting on the principle of transference or representation; maintaining law, and yet manifesting grace; declaring that "all have sinned and come short of the glory of God" (Romans 3:23); that "by the deeds of the law shall no flesh be justified in his sight, for by the law is the knowledge of sin" (Romans 3:20); yet presenting a divine Surety, "as a *propitiation* through faith in his blood, to declare his *righteousness* for the remission of sins that are past" (Romans 3:25).

Salvation by substitution was embodied in the first promise regarding the woman's seed and his bruised heel. Victory over our great enemy, by his subjecting himself to the bruising of that enemy, is then and there proclaimed. The clothing of our first parents with that which had passed through death, in preference to the fig-leaves which had not so done, showed the element of substitution as that on which God had begun to act in his treatment of fallen man. Abel's sacrifice revealed the same truth, especially as contrasted with Cain's. For that which made Abel's acceptable, and himself accepted, was the death of the victim as substituted for his own; that which rendered Cain's hateful, and himself rejected, was the absence of that death and blood. The slain firstling was accepted by God as, symbolically, Abel's substitute, laid on the altar till he should come; the "woman's seed," "made of a woman, made under the law, to redeem them that were under the law, that we might receive the adoption of sons" (Galatians 4:4–5).

From the beginning, God recognized this principle in his dealings with man: the just dying for the unjust and the blessed one becoming a curse that the cursed might be blessed. In all subsequent sacrifices it was the same. Noah's burnt offering was like Abel's, and Abraham's resembled Noah's. Transference of guilt from one who could not bear the penalty without being eternally lost, to one who could bear it and yet come forth from under it free and glorious—this was the deep truth into which God educated the patriarchs as that which lay at the foundation of his procedure with the sinner. The consumption of Abraham's sacrifice by the divine fire told him that the divine displeasure which should have rested on him forever had fallen upon a substitute and been exhausted so that there remained no more wrath, no darkness, "no condemnation" for him; nothing but deliverance and favor and everlasting blessedness.

But it was *the arrangements of the tabernacle* that brought out most fully this great principle of God's actings to the children of Adam.

In the passover blood, the idea was chiefly that of *protection* from peril. The lamb stood sentinel at the door of each family; the blood was their "shield and buckler." There might be trembling hearts within, wondering perhaps how a little blood could be so efficacious and make their dwelling so impregnable; disquieted, too, because they could not see the blood, but were obliged to be content with knowing that God saw it (Exodus 12:13). Yet no amount of fearfulness could alter the potency of that sprinkled blood, and no weakness of faith could make that God-given shield less efficacious against "the enemy and the avenger." The blood—the symbol of substitution—was on the lintel, and that was enough. They did not see it nor feel it, but *they knew that it was there;* and that sufficed. God saw it, and that was better than their seeing it. They were safe, and they knew that they were so. They could feast upon the lamb in peace, and eat their bitter herbs with thankful joy. They could sing by anticipation the Church's song, "If God be for us, who can be against us?"

But still it was not in Egypt, but in the wilderness; not in their paschal chamber, but in the sanctuary of their God that they were to learn the full and varied truth of pardon, cleansing, acceptance, and blessing through a substitute.

The old burnt offering of the patriarchs, on the footing of which these fathers had in ages past drawn near to God, was split into many parts. In the details of these we see the fulness and variety of the substitution.

The various sacrifices are all connected with the altar. Even that which was "burnt without the camp" was connected with the altar. It was no doubt carried forth without the camp and burnt with fire (Leviticus 6:30, 16:27); but "the blood was brought into the tabernacle of the congregation, to reconcile withal in the holy place." "The blood of the bullock was brought in, to make atonement in the holy place." Their connection with the altar is sufficient of itself to show the truth of substitution contained in them, for the altar was the place of transference. But in each of them we find something which expresses this more directly and fully.

In the *burnt offering* we see the perfection of the substitute presented in the place of our imperfection, in not loving God with all our heart.

In the *meat offering* we have the perfection of the substitute, as that on which, when laid upon the altar, God feeds, and on which he invites us to feed.

In the *peace offering* we find the perfection of the substitute laid on the same altar as an atonement, reconciling us to God; removing the distance and the enmity, and providing food for us out of that which had passed through death; for "he is our peace."

In the *sin offering* we see the perfection of the substitute whose blood is sprinkled on the altar and whose body is burnt without, as securing pardon for unconscious sins—sins of ignorance.

In the *trespass offering* there is the same perfection of the substitute in his atoning character procuring forgiveness for conscious and wilful sin.

In the *drink offering* we have the perfection of the substitute poured out on the altar as that by which God is refreshed and by which we are also refreshed. "His blood is drink indeed."

In the *incense* we have the "sweet savor" of the substitute going up to God in our behalf; the cloud of fragrance from his life and death with which God is well pleased, enveloping us and making us fragrant with a fragrance not our own; absorbing all in us that is displeasing or hateful and replacing it with a sweetness altogether perfect and divine.

In the *fire* we see the holy wrath of the Judge consuming the victim slain in the place of the sinner. In the *ashes* we have the proof that the wrath had spent itself, that the penalty was paid, that the work was done. "It is finished," was the voice of the ashes on the altar.

In all this we see such things as the following: (1) God's displeasure against sin; (2) that displeasure exhausted in a righteous way; (3) the substitute presented and accepted; (4) the substitute slain and consumed; (5) the transference of the wrath from the sinner to his representative; (6) God resting in his love over the sinner and viewing him in the perfection of his substitute; (7) the sinner recon-

ciled, accepted, complete, enjoying God's favor, and feeding at his
table on that on which God had fed; on that which had come from
the altar and had passed through the fire.

Thus God's acceptance of this principle, in his preparation of
acceptable worshippers for his sanctuary, shows the fitness and
value of it as well as the divine intention that it should be available
for the sinner in his drawing near to God. In this way it is that God
makes the sinner "perfect as pertaining to the conscience" (Hebrews
9:9), gives him "no more conscience of sins" (Hebrews 10:2), and
"purges his conscience from dead works to serve the living God"
(Hebrews 9:14). For that which satisfies the holiness of God cannot
but satisfy the conscience of the sinner. God, pointing to the altar,
says, "That is enough for me"; the sinner responds and says, "It is
enough for me."

As in the *Epistle to the Hebrews* we have this principle of
substitution applied to the sanctuary, so in that to the Romans we
find it applied to the courts of law. In the former we see God making
the sinner *perfect* as a worshipper; in the latter, *righteous* as a servant and a son. In the one it is priestly completeness; in the latter it
is judicial righteousness. But in both, the principle on which God
acts is the same. And as he acts on it in receiving us, so does he
invite us to act in coming to him.

It is this truth that the Gospel embodies, and it is this that we
preach when, as ambassadors for Christ, we pray men in Christ's
stead to be reconciled to God. God's free love to the sinner is the
first part of our message; God's righteous way of making that free
love available for the sinner is the second. What God is and what
Christ has done make up one Gospel. The belief of that Gospel is
eternal life. "All that believe are justified from all things" (Acts
13:39).

With a weak faith and a fearful heart many a sinner stands
before the altar. It is not the strength of his faith but the perfection
of the sacrifice that saves; and no feebleness of faith, no dimness of
eye, no trembling of hand, can change the efficacy of our burnt
offering. The vigor of our faith can add nothing to it, nor can the
poverty of it take anything from it. Faith, in all its degrees, still reads
the inscription, "The blood of Jesus Christ his Son cleanses us from
all sin." If at times the eye is so dim that it cannot read these words,
through blinding tears or bewildering mist, faith rests itself on the

certain knowledge of the fact that the inscription is still there, or at least that the blood itself (of which these words remind us) remains in all its power and suitableness upon the altar, unchanged and uneffaced. God says that the believing man is justified: Who are we, then, that we should say, "We believe, but we do not know whether we are justified?" What *God* has joined together, let not *man* put asunder.

The question as to the right way of believing is that which puzzles many and engrosses all their anxiety to the exclusion of the far greater questions as to the person and work of him who is the object of their believing. Thus their thoughts run in a self-righteous direction and are occupied, not with what *Christ has done*, but with what *they* have yet *to do* to get themselves connected with his work.

What should we have said to the Israelite, who, on bringing his lamb to the tabernacle, should puzzle himself with questions as to the right mode of laying his hands on the head of the victim and who should refuse to take any comfort from the sacrifice because he was not sure whether he had laid them aright—on the proper place, in the right direction, with adequate pressure, or in the best attitude? Should we not have told him that his own actings concerning the lamb were not the lamb, yet he was speaking as if they were? Should we not have told him that the lamb was everything and his touch nothing as to virtue or merit or recommendation? Should we not have told him to be of good cheer, not because he had laid his hands on the victim in the most approved fashion, but because they had touched that victim—however lightly and imperfectly—and thereby said, Let this lamb stand for me, answer for me, die for me? The touching had no virtue in itself. Therefore the excellency of the act was no question to come up at all: It simply intimated the man's desire that this sacrifice should be taken instead of himself as God's appointed way of pardon. It was simply the indication of his consent to God's way of saving him by the substitution of another. The point for him to settle was not, Was my touch right or wrong, light or heavy? but, Was it the touch of the right lamb—the lamb appointed by God for the taking away of sin?

The quality or quantity of faith is not the main question for the sinner. That which he needs to know is that Jesus died and was buried and rose again, according to the Scriptures. This knowledge is life everlasting.

3

THE COMPLETENESS OF THE SUBSTITUTION

In person and in work, in life and in death, Christ is the sinner's substitute. His vicariousness is co-extensive with the sins and wants of those whom he represents. It covers all the different periods as well as the varied circumstances of their lives.

He entered our world as the substitute. "There was no room for him in the inn" (Luke 2:7)—the inn of Bethlehem, the city of David, his own city. "Though rich, for our sakes he had become poor" (2 Corinthians 8:9). In poverty and banishment his life began. He was not to be allowed either to be born or to die, save as an outcast man. "Without the gate" (Hebrews 13:12) was his position as he entered and as he left our Earth. Man would not give even a roof to shelter or a cradle to receive the helpless babe. It was as the substitute that he was the outcast from the first moment of his birth. His vicarious life began in the manger. For what can this poverty mean, this rejection by man, this outcast condition, but that his sin-bearing had begun?*

The name, too, that met him as he came into our world intimated the same truth: "You shall call his name *Jesus,* for he shall save his people from their sins" (Matthew 1:21). His *name* proclaimed his mission and his work to be salvation; "Jehovah the Savior" (Jesus) is that by which the infant is called. As the *Savior,* he comes forth from the womb; as the *Savior,* he lies in the manger; and if he is the Savior, he is the substitute. The name *Jesus* was not given to him merely in reference to the cross, but to his whole life

---

*The Heidelberg Catechism (used in the Scotch Church, along with Calvin's, till superseded by the Westminster) asks, "What profit take you by Christ's holy conception and nativity?" and answers, "That he is our mediator, and covers my sins with his innocency and perfect holiness, in which I was conceived, that they may not come into the sight of God."

below. Therefore did Mary say, "My soul magnifies the Lord, and my spirit rejoices in God *my Savior*" (Luke 1:46, 47). Therefore also did the angel say to the shepherds, "Unto you is born this day, in the city of David, *a Savior,* which is Christ the Lord" (Luke 2:11).

Scarcely is he born when his blood is shed. Circumcision deals with him as one guilty and needing the sign of cleansing.* He knew no sin, yet he is circumcised. He was not born in sin nor shapen in iniquity, but was "the holy thing" (Luke 1:35); yet he is circumcised as other children of Abraham, for "he took upon him the seed of Abraham" (Hebrews 2:16). Why was he circumcised if not as the substitute? That rite proclaimed his vicarious birth as truly as did the cross his vicarious death. "He who knew no sin was made sin for us, that we might be made the righteousness of God in him" (2 Corinthians 5:21). This was the beginning of that obedience in virtue of which righteousness comes to us; as it is written, "As by one man's disobedience many were made sinners, so by the obedience of one shall many be made righteous" (Romans 5:19). For he himself testified concerning his baptism, "Thus it becomes us to fulfil all righteousness" (Matthew 3:15), and what was true of his baptism was no less so of his circumcision. The pain and the blood and the bruising of his tender body connected with that symbol of shame are inexplicable save on the supposition that even in infancy he was the vicarious one, not indeed bearing sin in the full sense and manner in which he bore it on the cross (for without *death,* sin-bearing could not have been consummated), but still bearing it in measure according to the condition of his years. Even then he was "the Lamb of God."

---

*"These ceremonial observances were so many confessions of sin. Christ, then, who was made sin for us, conformed to these" (Ames, *Medulla Theologica,* Book 1, ch. 21). "Hereby [by circumcision] he was represented to the world not only as a subject, but also as a sinner. For though he was pure and holy, yet this ordinance passing upon him seemed to imply as if corruption had indeed been in him, which must be cut off by mortification. . . . Thus was he represented as a sinner to the world, though most holy and pure in himself" (John Flavel, *Fountain of Life,* Sermon 19). "He was circumcised, and kept the law to deliver us from the condemnation of it. . . . Therefore we must seek our righteousness, not in the law, but in Christ, who hath fulfilled the same, and given us there his fulfilling" (Hugh Latimer on Matthew 2:1, 2).

His banishment into Egypt is referred to once and again by the old divines as part of that life of humiliation by which he was bearing our sins. As the banished one, he bore our banishment that we might return to God. He passed through Earth as an outcast, because he was standing in the outcast's place—"hurried up and down," says an old writer, "and driven out of his own land as a vagabond" (John Flavel). In each part of his sin-bearing life there is something to meet our case. By the first Adam we were made exiles from God and paradise; by the last Adam we are brought back from our wanderings, restored to the divine favor, and replaced in the paradise of God.

His baptism is the same in import with his circumcision. He needed not the symbol of death and cleansing, for he was wholly pure, and not liable to death on his own account. Why, then, should this sign of washing the unclean be applied to him if he was not then standing in the place of the unclean? What had water to do with the spotless one? What had "the figure of the putting away of the filth of the flesh, and of the answer of a good conscience toward God" (1 Peter 3:21), to do with him who had no filth of the flesh to put away and on whose conscience not the very shadow of dispeace had ever rested? But he was the substitute; into all the parts and circumstances of our life he enters, fulfilling all righteousness in the name of those whom he had come to save. The water was poured upon him as standing in our place and fulfilling our obligations.*

*The old hymns have not lost sight of those truths. As specimens, I give the following:

Stillat excisos pueri per artus	Efficacious blood drops from
Efficax noxas abolere sanguis;	The pierced limbs of the boy
Obligat morti pretiosa totum	To abolish punishments;
Stilla cruorem.	A precious drop requires the whole
	bloodshed to death.

Again:

Vix natus, ecce lacteum	Behold the infant, scarcely born,
Profundit Infans sanguinem,	Sheds the milk blood,
Libamen est hoc funeris	A sample of death,
Amoris hoc praeludium.	A prelude of love.

And again:

Dixit; et Patris veneratus iram	He spoke; and having respected
Sustinet vulnus silicis cruentae;	The wrath of the Father endures the

In the Psalms we find him giving utterance to his feelings while bearing sins that were not his own, but which were felt by him as if they were his own. Again and again he confesses sin. But what had the Holy One to do with confession or with strong crying and tears? What connection had he with the horrible pit and the miry clay, with the overwhelming floods and waves, with the deep waters, and the dust and the darkness, and the lowest pit? Why shrank he from the assembly of the wicked that enclosed him, from the "bulls that compassed him, the strong bulls of Bashan that beset him round," from the power of the dogs, from the sword, from the lion's mouth, from the horns of the unicorns? Why, during the days of his flesh, was he subjected to all this? And why were the powers of Earth and Hell let loose against him? Because he was the substitute who had taken our place, assumed our responsibilities, and undertaken to do battle with our enemies. In these Psalms we find the seed of the woman at war with the seed of the serpent and undergoing the varied anguish of the bruised heel.

He speaks not merely of the anguish of the *cross* when the full flood of wrath descended on him, but of his lifetime's daily griefs: "I am afflicted and ready to die *from my youth up:* I suffer your terrors, I am distracted" (Psalm 88:15). "My soul is full of troubles, my life draws nigh the grave," he said in the Psalms; just as afterwards he cried out, "My soul is exceeding sorrowful, even unto death." "My eye mourns by reason of affliction. . . . Your fierce wrath goes over me, your terrors have cut me off. . . . Lover and friend you have put far from me, and my acquaintance into darkness." Thus was he "despised and rejected of men" (*i.e. the* despised and rejected one of men), "a man of sorrows and acquainted with grief" (Isaiah 53:3). And of the meaning of all this we can have no doubt when we remember that he was always the sinless one bearing

	wound of the bloody rock;
Et jugum legis subit ipse, servis	And he himself submits to the yoke of the law
Ut juga demat.	In order to take away the yokes for his servants.

—Editor.

Little as these hymns contain of the finished work of the substitute, occasionally the great truth breaks out in connection with different events in the Lord's history.

our sins, carrying them *up to the cross* as well as bearing them *upon the cross* (1 Peter 2:24, ανήνεγκε); also that it is written of him, "Surely he has borne our griefs and carried our sorrows" (Isaiah 53:4); and yet again, that it is written expressly with reference to his daily life, "He healed all that were sick, that it might be fulfilled which was spoken by Esaias the prophet, saying, *he himself took our infirmities and bore our sicknesses*" (Matthew 8:17).* Vicariousness, or substitution, attached itself to each part of his life as truly as to his death.† Our burden he assumed when he entered the manger, and he laid it aside only at the cross. The utterance, "It is finished," pointed back to a whole life's sin-bearing work.

The confessions of our sins which we find in the Psalms (where, as "in a bottle," God has deposited the tears of the Son of man, Psalm 56:8) are the distinctest proofs of his work as the substitute. Let one example suffice: "O Lord, rebuke me not in your wrath, neither chasten me in your displeasure; for your arrows stick fast in me, and your hand presses me sore. There is no soundness in my flesh because of your anger; neither is there any rest in my bones because of my sin. For my iniquities are gone over my head; as an heavy burden, they are too heavy for me" (Psalm 38:1–4).

These confessions must be either those of the sinner or the sin bearer. They suit the former, and they show what views of sin we should entertain, and what our confessions should be. But they suit the latter no less. As they occur in those Psalms which are quoted in the New Testament as specially referring to Christ, we must take them as the confessions of the sin bearer, meant to tell us what *he* thought of sin when it was laid upon him simply as a substitute for others. The view thus given us of the completeness of the substitution is as striking as it is satisfying. We see here our Noah building

---

*The evangelist here translates directly from the Hebrew and differs from the Septuagint.

†The Heidelberg Catechism asks, "What do you believe when you say, *He suffered?*" and the answer is, "That he, all the time of his life which he led on Earth, but especially at the end thereof, sustained the wrath of God, both in body and soul, against the sin of mankind, that he might by his passion, as the only propitiatory sacrifice, deliver our body and soul from everlasting damnation, and purchase unto us the favor of God, righteousness, and everlasting life."

his wondrous ark for the salvation of his household. We see its beginning, middle, and end. We see its different parts, external and internal; each plank as it is laid; each nail as it is driven in. Its form is perfect; its structure in all details is complete; its strength and stability are altogether divine. Yet with what labor and amid what mockings is this ark constructed! Amid what strong crying and tears, what blood and agony, is it completed! Thus, however, we are assured of its perfection and security. Through the deep waters of this evil world it floats in peace. No storm can overset it, no billow break it nor so much as loosen one of its planks. They who have fled to it as a hiding place from the wind and a covert from the tempest are everlastingly safe.

When the Lord said, "Now is my soul troubled" (John 12:27); and when again he said, "My soul is exceeding sorrowful, even unto death" (Matthew 26:38), he spoke as the sin bearer. For what construction can we possibly put upon that trouble and sorrow but that they were for us?* Men, false to the great truth of a sin-bearing Christ, may say that in the utterance of this anguish he was merely giving us an example of patient endurance and self-sacrifice. But they who own the doctrine of Christ "suffering for sin, the just for the unjust," will listen to these bitter cries as to the very voice of the

---

*The old catechetical exposition of the Heidelberg Catechism brings this out fully: "The Godhead has so strengthened the human nature, and upheld it, that it could bear the weight of the wrath of God against sin. It has also given such dignity to the short sufferings of the human nature that it has satisfied for the eternal punishment which we had deserved. . . . What suffered he in his soul? Very heavy and terrible torments, anxieties, pains, sorrows, distresses, arising from the sense of God's wrath. . . . When and how long has Christ suffered? The whole time of his life which he led on Earth, but especially at the end thereof. The evangelical histories testify of banishments, Satan's temptations, poverty, disgrace, infirmities, hunger, thirst, fear, perils of life; especially in the garden of Gethsemane, in the judgment hall, on Golgotha. . . . He not only suffered for sin, but he felt God against him in that suffering as an angry judge. . . . Has he also purchased righteousness for us? Yes, so that the Father freely gives and bestows the same on us, and reckons it unto us; so that the satisfaction and righteousness of Christ being imputed to us, we may stand in God's judgment."

substitute and learn from the accomplishment of which he took our flesh, and lived our life, and died our death upon the tree.

But the completeness of the substitution comes out more fully at the cross. There the whole burden pressed upon him, and the wrath of God took hold of him, and the sword of Jehovah smote him; he poured out his soul unto death, and he was cut off out of the land of the living.

Then the work was done. "It is finished." The blood of the burnt offering was shed. The propitiation of God's wrath was made, the transgression finished, and the everlasting righteousness brought in.

All that follows is the fruit or result of the work *finished on the cross*. The grave is the awful pledge or testimony to his death as a true and real death, but it forms no part of the substitution or expiation.* Before our substitute reached the tomb, atonement had been completed. The resurrection is the blessed announcement of the Father that the work had been accepted and the substitute set free, but it was no part either of the atonement or the righteousness. The ascension and the appearing in the presence of God for us with his own blood are the carrying out of the atonement made upon Calvary, but they are no part of the expiation by means of which sin is forgiven and we are justified. All was finished, once and forever, when the substitute said, "Father, into your hands I commend my spirit."

There are some who would separate propitiation from the cross, who maintain that the three days' entombment was part of the sin-bearing. But the cry from the cross, "It is finished," silences all such theories. The altar is the only place of expiation, and it is *death* that is the wages of sin. Burial was but the visible proof of the reality of the death. The substitute's death once given instead of ours, the work is done. The fire has consumed the sacrifice. The ashes which remain are not the prolongation of that sacrifice, but the palpable proof that the fire has exhausted itself, that wrath is spent, and that nothing can now be added to or taken from the perfection of that sacrifice through which pardon and righteousness are henceforth to flow to the condemned and the ungodly.

---

*"To what end was he buried? That thereby he might make manifest that he was dead indeed" (Heidelberg Catechism).

"Justified by his *blood*" is the apostolic declaration; and, as the result of this, "saved from wrath through him" (Romans 5:9). Here we rest, sitting down beneath the shadow of the cross to receive the benefit of that justifying, saving, protecting sacrifice.

It is at and by the *cross* that God justifies the ungodly. "By his *stripes* we are healed" (Isaiah 53:5), and the symbol of the brazen serpent visibly declares this truth. It was the serpent when uplifted that healed the deadly bite, not the serpent after it was taken down and deposited in the tabernacle. As from that serpent—the figure of him who was "made a curse for us"—so from the *cross* health and life flow in. It is not resurrection but crucifixion that is the finishing of transgression and the making an end of sin.

"Reconciled to God by the *death* of his Son" (Romans 5:10) is another of the many testimonies to the value and efficacy of the cross. Reconciliation is not connected with resurrection. The "peace was made by the *blood of his cross*" (Colossians 1:20). The fruits and results of the peace offering may be many and various, but they are not the basis of reconciliation. That basis is the sacrificial blood-shedding. What can be more explicit than these three passages which announce justification by the blood, reconciliation by the death, and peace by "the blood of the cross"?

In the cross we see the priest and priesthood; in the resurrection, the king and royal power. To the priest belong the absolution and the cleansing and the justifying; to the king, the impartation of blessing to the absolved and the cleansed and the justified.

To the cross, therefore, do we look and cleave; knowing that out of its death life comes to us, and out of its condemnation, pardon and righteousness. With Christ were we crucified, and in this crucifixion we have "redemption through his blood, the forgiveness of sins, according to the riches of his grace."

Three times over in one chapter (Leviticus 1:9, 13, 17) we read these words, "It is a burnt sacrifice, an offering made by fire of a sweet savor unto the Lord." The apostle, referring to these words, says, "Christ has loved us, and has given himself for us, an offering and a sacrifice to God for a sweet-smelling savor" (Ephesians 5:2). This sweet savor came from the brazen altar, or altar of burnt-offering. It was the sweet odor of that sacrifice that ascended to God and that encompassed the worshiper so that he was covered all over with this sacrificial fragrance, presenting him *perfect* before God and making his own conscience feel that he was accepted as such and treated as such. Thus, by that burnt offering there is proclaimed to us justification in a crucified Christ.

The manifold blessings flowing from resurrection and ascension are not to be overlooked, but nowhere does Scripture teach *justification* by these. The one passage sometimes quoted to prove this declares the opposite (Romans 4:25), for the words truly translated run thus: "He was delivered *because we* had sinned, and raised again *because* of our justification." It was because the justifying work was *finished* that resurrection was possible. Had it not been so, he must have remained under the power of the grave. But the cross had completed the justification of his church. He was raised from the dead. Death could no longer have dominion over him. The work was finished, the debt paid, and the surety went forth free. He rose not in order to justify us, but because we were justified. In raising him from the dead, God the Father cleared him from the imputed guilt which had nailed him to the cross and borne him down to the tomb. "He was justified in the Spirit" (1 Timothy 3:16). His resurrection was not his justification, but the declaration that he was "justified." That resurrection in which we are one with him does not justify us, but proclaims that we were justified—justified by his blood and death.*

Insofar, then, as substitution is concerned, we have to do with the *cross* alone. It was, indeed, the place of *death,* but on that very account it was also to us the place of life and the pledge of resurrection.

The words of the apostle (Romans 6:6) are very explicit on this point: "Knowing this, that our old man has been crucified with him, that the body of sin might be destroyed, that henceforth we should not serve sin." Here we have three things connected directly with the *cross:* (1) The death of the old man; (2) the destruction of the

*"What other benefits do we receive by the sacrifice and death of Christ? That by virtue of his death our old man is crucified, slain, and buried together with him, that henceforth evil lusts and desires may not reign in us, but we may offer ourselves unto him a sacrifice of thanksgiving. . . . How does the resurrection of Christ profit us? First, by his resurrection he vanquished death, that he might make us partakers of that righteousness which he had purchased for us; secondly, we are stirred up by his power to a new life" (Heidelberg Catechism).

body of sin; (3) deliverance from the life-bondage of sin. Then he adds, "For he who dies is freed from sin" (verse 7). The word "freed" is literally "justified,"* teaching us that *death* is the exhaustion of the penalty and the justification of the sinner. Justification in a crucified Christ is the teaching of the Spirit here.

The words of another apostle are no less clear (1 Peter 4:1): "Christ suffered for us in the flesh; . . . he that has suffered in the flesh has ceased from sin." Here Christ on the cross is set before us, suffering, the just for the unjust. Having thus suffered, he has exhausted the penalty which he was bearing; and having exhausted it, his connection with sin has ceased: He is now in the state described elsewhere, "without sin" (Hebrews 9:28). The word "ceased" means more properly "has rest."† The life of our surety was one of sorrow and unrest, for our penalty lay upon him; but when this penalty was paid by his death, he "rested." The labor and the burden were gone; and as one who knew what entering into rest was (Hebrews 4:10), he could say to us, "I will give you *rest.*" He carried his life-long burden to the cross and there laid it down, "resting from his labors." Or rather, it was there that the law severed the connection between him and the burden, loosing it from his shoulders that it might be buried in his grave. From that same cross springs the sinner's rest, the sinner's disburdening, the sinner's absolution and justification.

Not for a moment are we to lose sight of the blessings flowing from resurrection or to overlook and undervalue the new position into which we are brought by it. The "power of his resurrection" (Philippians 3:10) must be fully recognized and acted on for its own results. We are crucified with Christ. With him we died, were buried, and rose again. "Raised with him through faith in the operation of God, who has raised him from the dead" (Colossians 2:2). "He has quickened us together with Christ, and has raised us up together, and made us sit together in heavenly places in Christ Jesus" (Ephesians 2:5–6). Such are the terms in which the apostle describes the benefits of Christ's resurrection and in which he reveals to us our oneness with him who died and rose. But nowhere does he separate

---

*δεδιχαίωτιλι, has been judicially released, legally set free, having paid the full penalty.

†See Kypke's *Observations in the New Testament,* who quotes some striking passages in classical Greek to illustrate this. See also Bengel and Winer.

our justification from the cross; nowhere does he speak of Christ meeting our legal responsibilities by his resurrection; nowhere does he ascribe to his resurrection that preciousness in whose excellency we stand complete. Acceptance and completeness in our standing before God are attributed to the cross and blood and death of the Divine Substitute.

Poor as my faith in this Substitute may be, it places me at once in the position of one to whom "God imputes righteousness without works." God is willing to receive me on the footing of his perfection; if I am willing to be thus received, in the perfection of another with whom God is well pleased, the whole transaction is completed. *I am justified by his blood.* "As he is, so am I (even) in *this* world"— even *now,* with all my imperfections and evils.

To be entitled to use another's name when my own name is worthless, to be allowed to wear another's raiment because my own is torn and filthy, to appear before God in another's person—the person of the Beloved Son—this is the summit of all blessing. The sin-bearer and I have exchanged names, robes, and persons! I am now represented by him, my own personality having disappeared. He now appears in the presence of God for me (Hebrews 9:24). All that makes him precious and dear to the Father has been transferred to me. His excellency and glory are seen as if they were mine. I receive the love and the fellowship and the glory as if I had earned them all. So entirely one am I with the sin bearer that God treats me not merely as if I had not done the evil that I have done, but as if I had done all the good which I have not done, but which my substitute has done. In one sense I am still the poor sinner, once under wrath; in another I am altogether righteous and shall be so forever because of the perfect one in whose perfection I appear before God. Nor is this a false pretence or a hollow fiction which carries no results or blessings with it. It is an exchange which has been provided by the Judge and sanctioned by law; an exchange of which any sinner upon earth may avail himself and be blest.

4

THE DECLARATION OF THE COMPLETENESS

The fifty-third chapter of Isaiah is a prophetic vision of the cross.

The book of Leviticus had given Israel in detail the standing symbols which were all to be transformed into spiritual substances or verities in Christ crucified. And this chapter of the prophet gives a summary of these truths in Levitical language, connecting them all with the seed of the woman and his bruising upon the tree.

For more than three thousand years the "bruised heel" had been held up before the eye of the world, and specially of Israel (in their sacrifices), as their deliverance and hope. But now the interpretation is given in more explicit language. Its meaning, as expressing (in the varied details of this chapter) the transference of the sinner's guilt to the substitute; as setting forth also the mysterious person of the man of sorrows, and, under all this, revealing the deep free love of God to man—is here proclaimed with a clearness and fulness such as had not hitherto been revealed either to the patriarchs or to Israel. Nowhere is the work of Messiah the sin bearer more explicitly revealed. The just one suffering for the unjust is the theme of this prophetic burden.

Abruptly the prophet breaks forth in his description of Messiah, seed of the woman, son of Adam, son of Abraham, son of David: "He shall grow up before him as a tender plant, and as a root out of a dry ground." The soil and the air of earth are alike uncongenial to this shoot from the stem of Jesse. Its affinities are all with a purer climate than ours.

He rises up in the midst of us, but not to be appreciated and honored, not to be admired or loved. "He has no form nor comeliness; and when we shall see him, there is no beauty that we should desire him." The light shines in the darkness, and the darkness comprehends it not. "He is [the] despised and rejected [one] of men," *i.e.* of all men, the most despised and rejected; for he came to his own, and his own received him not.

Here is the beginning of his vicarious life—a life of reproach among the sons of men, "a man of sorrows, and acquainted with grief."

Whence all this life-long sadness? When angels visit earth, are they thus sorrowful? Does the air of earth infect them with its troubles? Do they weep and groan and bleed? Are they assailed with the blasphemies of Earth? If not, why is it thus? Why is the holy Son of God from his childhood subjected to this contempt and bowed down beneath this burden? Why is the cup of gall and wormwood set beside his cradle? And why, day by day, in youth and manhood, has he to drink the bitter draught? Angels see the sights and hear the sounds of Earth as they attend us in their ministries or execute the errands of their King. Yet they are not saddened, nor when they return to their dwellings of light do they require the tears to be wiped from their eyes or the sweat from their brows. How can we account for the difference between Messiah and the angels, save by the fact that his sin-bearing character made him accessible to and penetrable by grief in a way such as no angel could be?

The difficulty of such a case was obvious, and accordingly the prophet meets it in the next verse. It was *our* griefs that he was bearing; it was *our* sorrows that he was carrying. These were the things that made him the man of sorrows. They that saw him could not understand the mystery. They said, God has smitten him for his sins and afflicted him for some hidden transgression that we know not. But no: "He was wounded for *our* transgressions, he was bruised for *our* iniquities; the chastisement of *our* peace was upon him, and with his stripes *we* are healed." The wounding, the bruising, the chastening, and the scourging had their beginnings before he reached the cross; but it was there that they were all completed by "the obedience unto *death*."

"The Lord [Jehovah] has laid on him the iniquity of us all," or, has made to rush or strike upon him the punishment of us all.

> It was exacted, and he became answerable,
> And [therefore] he opened not his mouth.
> As a lamb to the slaughter he is led;
> And as a sheep before her shearers is dumb,

So he opened not his mouth.
From prison and from judgment he is taken,
And his generation [manner of life] who declares?

These are scenes *before the cross,* while he was on his way to it. He was silent before his judges because he had made himself legally responsible for our debt or guilt. Nor was there anyone to come forward and declare his innocence. He was carrying, too, our sins to the cross. After this we have the cross itself:

He was cut off out of the land of the living;
For the transgression of my people was he stricken.

The sin bearing of the cross is fully brought out here. There he hung as the substitute, "the just for the unjust, that he might bring us to God."

And there was appointed him a grave with the wicked,
But with the rich man was he in death.

There was assigned to him a place with the wicked not only on the cross, but in his burial; he was condemned not only to die an ignominious death, but to have a like sepulchre. From this latter, however, he was delivered by the rich man of Arimathea who unexpectedly came forward and begged the body, which would otherwise have been consigned to a malefactor's grave. He was "with the rich in his death"; that is, when he died, or after his death, when he was taken down from the cross.

Yet it pleased Jehovah to bruise him,
He has put him to grief.

Jehovah was well pleased with his bruising—nay, took pleasure in bruising him. Never was Messiah more the "beloved Son" than when suffering on the cross; yet Jehovah was "well pleased" to put him to grief. Though the *consciousness* of communion was interrupted for a time when he cried, "Why have you forsaken me?" yet there was no breaking of the bond. There was *wrath* coming down on him as the *Substitute,* but *love* resting on him as the *Son.* Both were together. He knew the love, even while he felt the wrath. It was the knowledge of the love that made him cry out in amazement and anguish, "My God, my God, why have you forsaken me?"

You shall make his soul an offering for sin;

or more exactly, "a trespass offering"; a sacrifice for wilful, conscious sin. Of this trespass offering it is written, "The priest shall make an atonement for him before the Lord, and he shall be forgiven for anything that he has done in trespassing therein" (Leviticus 6:7). The various offerings of the tabernacle and the altar all center in and cluster round the cross. It is *the soul* that is here said to be the trespass offering, implying that when the soul was parted from the body—when Christ commended his spirit to his Father—then the trespass offering was completed. Atonement was made once for all. Before the body of the surety had reached the tomb, the great work was done. The lying in the grave was the visible and palpable sign or pledge of the work having been *already finished;* resurrection was the Father's seal from above set to the excellency of that completed sacrifice and to the perfection of him by whom it had been accomplished on the cross.

Upon the labor of his *soul* he shall look,
He shall be satisfied.

Christ, in the days of his flesh, often used language like this regarding his *soul:* "My *soul* is exceeding sorrowful, even unto *death*" (Matthew 26:38); "Now is my *soul* troubled" (John 12:27); "The Son of man came . . . to give his *soul* a random for many" (Matthew 20:28); "The good Shepherd gives his *soul* for the sheep" (John 10:11); "I lay down my *soul* for the sheep" (John 10:15). Thus the life, the soul, the blood, are connected together; and with that which was accomplished by them in life and in death he is *satisfied*. Whether it is *himself* that is satisfied, or the Father, matters not. The truth taught is the same.

By his knowledge shall my righteous Servant justify many;
For he shall bear their iniquities.

It is the Father that here speaks. He calls Messiah, "My righteous servant," and proclaims that by giving the knowledge of himself he shall justify many. The knowledge of Christ is that which secures our justification; the knowledge of Christ as the *sin bearer*. For it is added, as the *justifying thing* in this knowledge, "he shall bear their iniquities"; thus again linking justification with the cross, and the finished work there.

The last verse is very remarkable as bringing out fully the Father's reasons for glorifying his Son, reasons connected entirely with the cross and the sin bearing there:

Therefore will I divide him a portion with the great,
And he shall divide the spoil with the strong,
Because he has poured out his soul unto death.
And he was numbered with the transgressors;
And he bore the sin of many,
And made intercession for the transgressors.

So that the resurrection, with all the subsequent glory and honor conferred on him, is the recompense and result of his justifying work upon the cross. On that tree of death and shame the work was *finished*. There he poured out his soul; there he was numbered with the transgressors; there he bore the sin of many; there he made intercession for the transgressors when he cried out, "Father, forgive them, for they know not what they do."*

"It is finished," were his words as he died. The justifying work is done! If anything else besides this finished work is to justify, then Christ has died in vain.

"It is finished," he said, and gave up the ghost. "Father, into your hands I commend my spirit," and to the Father that spirit went. The Father received it, and, in receiving it, bore testimony to the completeness of the work. The Roman soldiers, "perceiving that he was dead already," may be said to have testified to the completion of the work of pouring out his soul unto death. The taking down from the cross was another testimony. Joseph and Nicodemus were like the Levites carrying away the ashes from the altar.

---

*In these words, "they know not what they do," he is speaking as the *sin offering*, which was specially for sins of ignorance.

The burial was another testimony. The resurrection began the divine and visible testimony to this same thing. The ascension and "sitting" at the Father's right hand were the attestations from above—the heavenly responses to the voice from the cross, "It is finished." All after this was the *result* of that finished work. The presentation of his blood was not to complete the sacrifice, but to carry out what was already done. The sprinkling of the blood (at whatever time that may have been done) was the application of the sacrifice, not the sacrifice itself.

"It is finished!" He who makes this announcement on the cross is the Son of God; it is he who but the day before had said in the prospect of this consummation, "I have glorified you on the Earth, I have finished the work which you gave me to do." He knows what he says when he utters it, and he is "the faithful and true witness." His words are true, and they are full of meaning.

He makes this announcement before the Father as if calling on him to confirm it. He makes it before Heaven and Earth, before men and angels, before Jew and Gentile. He makes it to us. Listen, O sons of men! The work that saves is perfected. The work that justifies is done.

The completeness thus announced is a great and momentous one. It is one in which all the ends of the Earth have an interest. Had ought been left unfinished, then what hope for man or for man's Earth? But it is begun, carried on, consummated. No flaw is found in it; no part is left out; not a jot or tittle has failed. It is absolutely perfect.

This perfection or consummation of the Father's purpose is the completion of atonement, the completion of the justifying work, the completeness of the sin bearing and law fulfilling, the completeness of the righteousness, the completeness of the covenant and the covenant seal. All is done, and done by him who is Son of man and Son of God. It is perfectly and forever done; nothing to be added to it or taken from it by man, by Satan, or by God. The burial of the substitute does not add to its completeness; resurrection forms no part of that justifying work. It was all concluded on the cross.

It is so finished that a sinner may at once use it for pardon, for rest, for acceptance, for justification. Standing beside this altar where the great burnt offering was laid and consumed to ashes, the sinner feels that he is put in possession of all blessing. That which the altar has secured passes over to him simply in virtue of his taking his place at the altar and thus identifying himself with the victim. There the divine displeasure against sin has spent itself; there righteousness has been obtained for the unrighteous; there the sweet savor of rest is continually ascending before God; there the full flood of divine love is ever flowing out; there God meets the sinner in his fullest grace without hindrance or restraint; there the peace which has been made through blood-shedding is found by the sinner; there reconciliation is proclaimed, and the voice that proclaims it from that altar reaches to the ends of the Earth; there the ambassadors of peace take their stand to discharge their embassy, pleading with the sons of men far off and near, saying, "Now then we are ambassadors for Christ, as though God did beseech you by us; we pray you in Christ's stead, be reconciled to God."

The resurrection was the great visible seal set to this completeness. It was the Father's response to the cry from the cross, "It is finished." As at baptism he spoke from the excellent glory and said, "This is my beloved Son, in whom I am well pleased," so did he speak (though not with audible voice) at the resurrection, bearing testimony thereby not only to the excellency of the person, but to the completeness of the work of his only begotten Son. The resurrection added nothing to the propitiation of the cross; it proclaimed it already perfect, incapable of addition or greater completeness.

The ascension added to this testimony, especially the sitting at God's right hand. "This man, after he had offered one sacrifice for sins forever, *sat down* at the right hand of God" (Hebrews 10:12). "When he had by himself purged our sins, *sat down* on the right hand of the Majesty on high" (Hebrews 1:3). The standing posture of the ancient priests showed that their work was an unfinished one. The *sitting down* of our high priest intimated to all Heaven that the work was done and the "eternal redemption obtained." And what was thus intimated in Heaven has been proclaimed on Earth by those whom God sent forth in the power of the Holy Ghost to tell to men the things which eye had not seen nor ear heard. That "sitting down" contained in itself the Gospel. The first note of that Gospel was sounded at Bethlehem from the manger where the young child lay: The last note came from the throne above when the Son of God returned in triumph from his mission of grace to Earth and took his seat upon the right hand of the Majesty in the heavens.

Between these two extremities—the manger and the throne—
how much is contained for us! All the love of God is there. The
exceeding riches of divine grace are there. The fulness of that power
and wisdom and righteousness which have come forth, not to destroy but to save, is there. These are the two boundary walls of that
wondrous storehouse out of which we are to be filled throughout the
eternal ages.

Of what is contained in this treasure house we know something
here in some small measure, but the vast contents are beyond all
measurement and all conception. The eternal unfolding of these to
us will be perpetual gladness. Apart from the excellency of the
inheritance and the beauty of the city—and the glory of the kingdom—which will make us say, "Truly the lines have fallen unto us
in pleasant places,"—there will be, in our ever-widening knowledge
of "the unsearchable riches of Christ," light and replenishment and
satisfaction which, even were all external brightnesses swept away,
would be enough for the soul throughout all the ages to come.

The present glory of Christ is the reward of his humiliation
here. Because he humbled himself and became obedient unto death,
even the death of the cross, God has highly exalted him and given
him the name that is above every name. He wears the crown of glory
because he wore the crown of thorns. He drank of the brook by the
way; therefore, he has lifted up the head (Psalm 110:7).

But this is not all. That glory to which he is now exalted is the
standing testimony before all Heaven that his work was finished on
the cross. "I have finished the work which you gave me to do," he
said. Then he added, "Now, O Father, glorify me with your own
self, with the glory which I had with you before the world was"
(John 17:4, 5).

The proofs of the completeness of the sacrificial work upon the
cross are very full and satisfying. They assure us that the work was
really finished and, as such, available for the most sinful of men.
We shall find it good to dwell upon the thought of this completeness
for the pacifying of the conscience, for the satisfying of the soul, for
the removal of all doubt and unbelief, and for the production and
increase of faith and confidence.

There are *degrees of rest* for the soul, and it is in proportion as
we comprehend the perfection of the work on Calvary that our rest
will increase. There are *depths of peace* which we have not yet

sounded, for it is "peace which passes all understanding." Into these depths the Holy Spirit leads us, not in some miraculous way or by some mere exertion of power, but by revealing to us more and more of that work in the first knowledge of which our peace began.

We are never done with the cross nor ever shall be. Its wonders will be always new and always fraught with joy. "The Lamb as it had been slain" will be the theme of our praise above. Why should such a name be given to him in such a book as the Revelation, which in one sense carried us far past the cross, were it not that we shall always realize our connection with its one salvation; we shall always be looking to it even in the midst of the glory; and we shall always be learning from it some new lesson regarding the work of him "in whom we have redemption through his blood, even the forgiveness of sins, according to the riches of his grace"? What will they who here speak of themselves as being so advanced as to be done with the cross say to being brought face to face with the slain Lamb, in the age of absolute perfection, the age of the heavenly glory?

You fool! Do you not know that the cross of the Lord Jesus Christ endures forever and that you shall eternally glory in it, if you are saved by it at all?

You fool! Will you not join in the song below, "To him who loved us, and washed us from our sins in his own blood"? Will you not join in the song above, "You were slain, and here redeemed us to God by your blood"? And do you not remember that it is from "the Lamb as it had been slain" that "the seven spirits of God are sent forth into all the Earth"? (Revelation 5:6.)*

It is *the Lamb* who stands in the midst of the elders (Revelation 5:6) and before whom they fall down. "Worthy is *the Lamb*" is the theme of celestial song. It is *the Lamb* that opens the seals (6:1). It is before *the Lamb* that the great multitude stand clothed in white (7:9). It is the blood of *the Lamb* that washes the raiment white (7:14). It is by the blood of *the Lamb* that the victory is won (12:11). The book of life belongs to the *Lamb slain* (13:8). It was the *Lamb* that stood on the glorious Mount Zion (14:1). It is *the Lamb* that the

---

*Thirty times does the word *Lamb*, as Christ's heavenly name, occur in the Apocalypse; bringing perpetually before the redeemed in glory the cross and the blood as if to prevent the possibility of our losing sight of *Christ crucified*.

redeemed multitude are seen following (14:4), and that multitude is the first fruits unto God and unto *the Lamb* (14:4). It is the song of *the Lamb* that is sung in heaven (15:3). It is *the Lamb* that wars and overcomes (17:14). It is the marriage of *the Lamb* that is celebrated, and it is to the marriage supper of the *Lamb* that we are called (19:7, 9). The church is *the Lamb's* wife (21:9). On the foundations of the heavenly city are written the names of the twelve apostles of *the Lamb* (21:14). Of this city the Lord God Almighty and *the Lamb* are the temple (21:22). Of that city *the Lamb* is the light (21:23). The book of life of *the Lamb* and the throne of *the Lamb* (21:27, 22:1, 3) sum up this wondrous list of honors and dignities belonging to the Lord Jesus as the *crucified* Son of God.

Thus the glory of Heaven revolves around the cross, and every object on which the eye lights in the celestial city will remind us of the cross and carry us back to Golgotha. Never shall we get beyond it, or turn our backs on it, or cease to draw from it the divine virtue which it contains.

The tree—be it palm, cedar, or olive—can never be independent of its roots, however stately its growth and however plentiful its fruit. The building—be it palace or temple—can never be separated from its foundation, however spacious or ornate its structure may be. So, never shall the redeemed be independent of the cross or cease to draw from its fulness.

In what ways our looking to the cross hereafter will benefit us; what the shadow of that tree will do for us in the eternal kingdom, I know not, nor do I venture to say. But it would seem as if the cross and the glory were so inseparably bound together that there cannot be the enjoyment of the one without the remembrance of the other. The completeness of the sacrificial work on Calvary will be matter for eternal contemplation and rejoicing long after every sin has been, by its cleansing efficacy, washed out of our being forever.

Shall we ever exhaust the fulness of the cross? Is it a mere stepping-stone to something beyond itself? Shall we ever cease to glory in it (as the apostle gloried), not only because of past, but because of present and eternal blessing? The forgiveness of sin is one thing, but is that all? The crucifixion of the world is another, but is that all? Is the cross to be a relic, useless though venerable, like the serpent of brass laid up in the tabernacle to be destroyed perhaps at some future time and called Nehushtan? (2 Kings 18:4).

Or is it not rather like the tree of life which bears twelve manner of fruits and yields its fruit every month by the banks of the celestial river? Its influence here on Earth is transforming. But even after the transformation has been completed and the whole church perfected, shall there not be a rising higher and higher, a taking on of greater and yet greater comeliness, a passing from glory to glory—all in connection with the cross and through the never-ending vision of its wonders?

Of the new Jerusalem it is said, "The *Lamb* is the light [or lamp] thereof" (Revelation 21:23). The Lamb is only another name for *Christ crucified*. Thus it is the cross that is the lamp of the holy city; and with its light the gates of pearl, the jasper wall, the golden streets, the brilliant foundations, and the crystal river are all lighted up. The glow of the cross is everywhere, penetrating every part, reflected from every gem; and by its peculiar radiance transporting the dwellers of the city back to Golgotha as the fountainhead of all this splendor.

It is light from Calvary that fills the Heaven of heavens. Yet it is no dim religious light, for the glory of God is to lighten it (Revelation 21:23). Its light is "like unto a stone most precious, even like a jasper stone, clear as crystal . . . . and there is no night there, and they need no candle, neither light of the sun, for the Lord God gives them light" (Revelation 21:11;22:5). Yes, we shall never be done with the cross and the blood; though, where all are clean and perfect in every sense, these will not be used for purging the conscience or justifying the ungodly.

It is the symbol both of a dying and of a risen Christ that we find in the Revelation. The "Lamb as it had been slain" indicates both. But the prominence is given to the former. It is the slain Lamb that has the power and authority to open the seals; implying that it was in his sin bearing or sacrificial character that he exercised his right, and that it was his finished work on which this right rested and by which it was acquired. It is as the Lamb that he is possessed with all wisdom and strength—"the seven horns and the seven eyes, which are the seven Spirits of God" (Revelation 5:6); the Holy Spirit, or the Spirit of omniscience and omnipotence.

The Lamb is one of his special and eternal titles; the name by which he is best known in Heaven. As such, we obey and honor and worship him; never being allowed to lose sight of the cross amid all the glories of the kingdom. As such we follow him, and shall follow him eternally. As it is written, "There are they that follow *the Lamb* wherever he goes" (Revelation 14:4).

5

RIGHTEOUSNESS FOR THE UNRIGHTEOUS

It is *in* righteousness and *by* righteousness that God saves the sinner.

He justifies the ungodly (Romans 4:5), but he does it *in* and *by* *righteousness*. For "the righteous Lord loves righteousness" (Psalm 11:7). He "justifies *freely* by his *grace*" (Romans 3:24), but still it is "in and by righteousness." His grace is *righteous* grace; it is grace which condemns the sin while acquitting the sinner; nay, which condemns the sin by means of that very thing which brings about the acquittal of the sinner. His pardon is *righteous* pardon and therefore irreversible. His salvation is *righteous* salvation and therefore everlasting.

It is as the righteous *Judge* that God justifies. He is "faithful and just" in forgiving sin (1 John 1:9). By his pardons he magnifies his righteousness, so that he who goes to God for forgiveness can use as his plea the righteousness of the righteous Judge, no less than the grace of the loving and merciful Lord God.

God loves to pardon because he is love; and he loves to pardon because he is righteous, and true, and holy. No sin can be too great for pardon, and no sinner can be too deep or old in sin to be saved and blest because the righteousness out of which the salvation comes is infinite.*

---

*"How are you righteous before God? Only by a true faith in Jesus Christ: insomuch that if my conscience accuse me that I have grievously transgressed against all the commandments of God, nor have kept any one of them, and, moreover, am still prone to evil; yet, notwithstanding, *the full and perfect satisfaction, righteousness, and holiness of Christ is imputed and given to me,* without any merit of mine, of the mere mercy of God, even as if I had never committed any sin, or as if no spot at all did cleave to me, yea, as if I myself had perfectly performed that obedience which Christ performed for me. . . .

The sacrifices on which the sinner is called to rest are "the sacrifices of *righteousness*" (Deuteronomy 33:19; Psalm 4:5). It is from "the God of our salvation" that this *righteousness* comes (Psalm 24:5). It is with the "sacrifices of *righteousness*" that God is "pleased" (Psalm 51:19). It is with *righteousness* that his *priests* are clothed (Psalm 132:9). It is *righteousness* that looks down from Heaven to bless us (Psalm 85:11), and it is *righteousness* and *peace* that kiss each other in bringing deliverance to our world. It is the work of *righteousness* that is *peace*, and "the effect of *righteousness*, quietness, and assurance forever*" (Isaiah 32:17).

It is with the "robe of *righteousness*" that Messiah is clothed, over and above the garments of salvation (Isaiah 61:10), when he comes to deliver Earth. When he proclaims himself "mighty to save," it is when "speaking in *righteousness*" (Isaiah 63:1). When he came to "finish the transgression, and to make an end of sin, and to make reconciliation for iniquity," he came also to bring in "everlasting *righteousness*" (Daniel 9:24).

"This is the name whereby he shall be called, *The Lord our righteousness*" (Jeremiah 23:6); and as if to mark the way in which he blesses and justifies, it is added in another place, "This is the name wherewith *she* shall be called, The Lord our righteousness" (Jeremiah 33:16)—his name passing over to the sinner, with the sinner's name lost and forgotten in that of his substitute. Oneness in name, in nature, in privilege, in position, in righteousness, and in glory with Messiah his divine sinbearer is the sinner's portion. "Their *righteousness* is of *me*, says the Lord" (Isaiah 54:17); for "he, of God, is made unto us *righteousness*" (1 Corinthians 1:30). The transference is complete and eternal. From the moment that we receive the divine testimony to the righteousness of the Son of God,

---

Why is Christ's sacrifice and obedience called the material cause of our justification? For that it is the same for which we are made righteous (Romans 5:19).—Is Christ's death and last passion only imputed to us, or also the obedience of His life? Both. His satisfaction by punishment merits for us the remission of sin. This is his *passive* obedience. Then there is the obedience called *active* obedience. . . . We owed to God not only punishment for the transgression, but also a perfect obedience. All this Christ has satisfied for us. But our justification is most ascribed to Christ's suffering, blood-shedding, and death" (Heidelberg Catechism).

all the guilt that was on us passes over to him, and all his righteousness passes over to us, God looks on us as possessed of that righteousness and treats us according to its value in his sight. Men may call this a mere "name" or "legal fiction," but it is such a "name" as secures for us the full favor of the righteous God who can only show favor to us in a righteous way. It is such a "fiction" as law recognizes and God acts upon in dealing with the unrighteous as if they were righteous—supremely and divinely righteous in virtue of their connection with him who, "though he knew no sin, was made sin for us, that we might be made the *righteousness of God* in him" (2 Corinthians 5:21).

This is "the righteousness of God which is revealed from faith to faith" (Romans 1:17).* This is "the righteousness of God without the law which is manifested and was witnessed by the law and the prophets," (Romans 3:21); "the righteousness of God which is by faith of Jesus Christ unto all and upon all them that believe" (Romans 3:22).† Thus, "in believing" (not in doing) this "righteousness of God" becomes ours; for the promise of it is "to him that works not, but believes on him that justifies the ungodly" (Romans 4:5).

On our part there is the "believing"; on God's part, the "imputing" or reckoning. We believe; he imputes; and the whole transaction is done. The *blood* (as "atoning" or "covering") washes off our guilt. The *righteousness* presents us before God as legally entitled to that position of righteousness which our surety holds; as being himself not merely the righteous one, but "Jehovah *our* righteousness." We get the benefit of his perfection in all its completeness, not as infused into us, but as covering us: "Your beauty was perfect through *my comeliness* which I had put upon you (Ezekiel 16:14). Applying here the words of the prophet concerning Jerusalem, we

---

*That is, "Therein is the righteousness of God, which is by faith, revealed to be believed."

†That is, the righteousness which God has provided for us—the righteousness of him who is God and which comes to us by believing in Christ—is presented to all without distinction and is put upon all who believe for a robe or covering. As it is written, *"Put on* the Lord Jesus Christ" (Romans 13:14), and again, "As many of you as have been baptized into Christ have *put on* Christ" (Galatians 3:27).

may illustrate and extend the figure used by the Holy Spirit as to the "perfection" of him whom this righteousness covers. Spread out, it is as follows:

1. "I said to you, 'Live'" (Ezekiel 16:6).
2. "I spread my skirt over you" (16:8).
3. "I entered into a covenant with you, and you became mine" (16:8).
4. "I washed you" (16:9).
5. "I anointed you" (16:9).
6. "I clothed you" (16:10).
7. "I shod you" (16:10).
8. "I girded you" (16:10).
9. "I covered you with silk" (16:10).
10. "I decked you with ornaments, bracelets, chains, jewels, a beautiful crown" (16:11–12).
11. "You were exceedingly beautiful" (16:13).
12. "Your renown went forth for your beauty" (16:14).

Such, in the symbols of Scripture, is a picture of the perfection (not our own) with which we are clothed so soon as we believe in him who is "Jehovah our righteousness." "You are all fair, my love; there is no spot in you" (Song of Solomon 4:7).

"He that believes is not condemned" (John 3:18). This is the negative side; even were there no more for us, this would be blessedness, seeing our portion was by nature that of "children of wrath." But there is more, for it is written, "All that believe are justified from all things" (Acts 13:39); and "Christ is the end [or fulfilling] of the law for righteousness to every one that believes" (Romans 10:4). "As by the offence of one, judgment came upon all men to condemnation; even so by *the righteousness of one*, the free gift came upon all men into *justification of life*" (Romans 5:18).

The strength or kind of faith required is nowhere stated. The Holy Spirit has said nothing as to quantity or quality on which so many dwell and over which they stumble, remaining all their days in darkness and uncertainty. It is simply in *believing*—feeble as our faith may be—that we are invested with this righteousness. For faith is not work, nor merit, nor effort, but the cessation from all these and the acceptance in place of them of what another has done—done completely and forever. The simplest, feeblest faith suffices: It is not the excellence of our act of faith that does anything for us, but

the excellence of him who suffered for sin—the just for the unjust—
that he might bring us to God. His perfection suffices to cover not
only that which is imperfect in our characters and lives, but that
which is imperfect in our faith when we believe on his name.

Many a feeble hand—perhaps many a palsied one—was laid
on the head of the burnt offering (Leviticus 1:4), but the feebleness
of that palsied touch did not alter the character of the sacrifice or
make it less available in all its fulness for him who brought it. The
priest would not turn him away from the door of the tabernacle
because his hand trembled, nor would the bullock fail to be "accepted for him, to make atonement for him" (Leviticus 1:4) because
his fingers might barely touch its head by reason of his feebleness.
The burnt offering was still the burnt offering. The weakest touch
sufficed to establish the connection between it and him. Even that
feeble touch was the expression of his consciousness that he was
unfit to be dealt with on the footing of what he was himself and of
his desire to be dealt with by God on the footing of another, infinitely worthier and more perfect than himself.

On our part there is unrighteousness, condemning us: On God's
part there is righteousness, forgiving and blessing us. Thus unrighteousness meets righteousness, not to war with each other, but to
be at peace. They come together in love, not in enmity. The hand
of righteousness is stretched out not to destroy, but to save.

It is as the *unrighteous* that we come to God; not with goodness
in our hands as a recommendation, but with the utter want of goodness; not with amendment or promises of amendment, but with *only
evil*, both in the present and the past; not presenting the claim of
contrition or repentance or broken hearts to induce God to receive
us as something less than unrighteous, but going to him simply as
unrighteous; and unable to remove that unrighteousness or offer
anything either to palliate or propitiate.*

---

*"I may boldly glory of all the victory which he obtains over the law, sin,
death, the devil; and may challenge to myself all his works, even as if they
were my own, and I myself had done them. . . . Wherefore, when the law shall
come and accuse you that you do not observe it, send it to Christ, and say,
'There is that man who has fulfilled the law; to him I cleave; he has fulfilled it
for me, and has given his fulfilling unto me.' When it hears these things, it will

It is the conscious absence of all good things that leads us to the fountain of all goodness. That fountain is open to all who thus come; it is closed against all who come on any other footing. It is the want of light and life that draws us to the one source of both, and both of these are the free gifts of God.

He who comes as partly righteous is sent empty away. He who comes acknowledging unrighteousness but at the same time trying to neutralize it or to expiate it by feelings, prayers, and tears, is equally rejected. But he who comes as an *unrighteous* man to a *righteous* yet *gracious* God, finds not only ready access, but plenteous blessing. The righteous God receives unrighteous man if man presents himself in his own true character as a sinner and does not mock God by pretending to be something less or better than this.

---

be quiet. If sin come, and would have you by the throat, send it to Christ, and say, 'As much as you may do against him, so much right shall you have against me; for I am in him, and he is in me.' If death creep upon you and attempt to devour you, say unto it, 'Good mistress Death, do you know this man? Come, bite out his tooth: Have you forgotten how little your biting prevailed with him once? Go to! If it be a pleasure unto you, encounter him again. You have persuaded yourself that you should have prevailed somewhat against him when he did hang between two thieves, and died an ignominious death; but what did you gain thereby? You did bite, indeed, but it turned worst to yourself. I pertain to this man; I am his and he is mine, and where he abides I will abide. You could not hurt him; therefore let me alone. . . .'

Hereof we may easily understand what kind of works those be which make us entire and righteous before God. Surely they are the works of another. . . . Salvation has come unto all by Jesus Christ, as by the works of another. Wherefore this is diligently to be noted: Our felicity does not consist in our own works, but in the works of another, namely, of Christ Jesus our Savior, which we obtain through faith only in him. . . . 'Before God your righteousness is of no estimation. You must set in place thereof another, namely mine. This God my Father allows. I have appeased the wrath of God, and of an angry Judge have made him a gentle, merciful, and gracious Father. Believe this, and it goes well with you; you are then safe, entire, and righteous. Beware that you presume not to deal before God with your own works. But if you will do anything with him, creep into me, put on me, and you shall obtain of my Father whatever you desire.'"

—Martin Luther, Sermon on John 20:24–29.

For then the divinely provided righteousness comes in to cover the unrighteous and to enable God to receive him in love and justify him before Earth and Heaven.

In all this we find such things as the following—each of them bringing out a separate aspect of the answer to the great question, "How can man be just with God?"

1. The Justifier—"it is God that justifies." The sentence of acquittal must come from *his* lips and be registered in his books.

2. The justified—man, the sinner, under wrath, the ungodly, the condemned.

3. The justifying fact—the death of him whose name is Jehovah our righteousness.

4. The justifying instrument—faith. Not strong faith, or great faith, or perfect faith, but simply faith, or believing. "We are justified by faith."

5. The justifying medium—the righteousness of God. This is the "best robe" which is prepared for the prodigal. By it he is clothed, beautified, made fit to enter his Father's house, and sit down at his Father's table. Christ is himself our justification. In him we "stand." In him we are "found." Him we "put on"; with him we are clothed; by him we are protected as by a shield; in him we take refuge as in a strong tower.

"Found in Him." What then? Our own "self" has disappeared; instead there is Christ, the beloved Son in whom God is well pleased. Found in ourselves, there was nothing but wrath; found in him, there is nothing but favor. We are hidden in Christ. God seeks for us; when at last he discovers us in our hiding-place, it is not *we* that he finds, but Christ, so complete is the exchange of persons, so perfect and so glorious the disguise. Yet it is not a disguise which shall ever be taken off, nor of which we shall have cause to be ashamed. It remains ours forever. It is an everlasting righteousness.*

---

*In this there is no confusion of personalities; no transfer of moral character; no exchange of *inherent* sin on the one hand or *inherent* righteousness on the other; no literal or physical identity. Rather a judicial verdict or sentence is given in our favor, constituting us *partakers in law* of all the results or fruits of the work of him whom God, as Judge, appointed our substitute. "As we are

Jehovah is satisfied with Christ's obedience. He is well-pleased with his righteousness. And when we, crediting his testimony to that obedience and that righteousness, consent to be treated by him on the footing of its perfection, then is he satisfied and well-pleased with us.

Jehovah is satisfied—more than satisfied—with Christ's fulfilling of the law which man had broken. For never had that law been so fulfilled in all its parts as it was in the life of the God-man. For man to fulfil it would have been much; for an angel to fulfil it would have been more, but for him who was God and man to fulfil it was yet unspeakably more. So satisfied is Jehovah with this divine law-fulfilling, and with him who so gloriously fulfilled it, that he is willing to pass from or cancel all the law's sentences against us; nay, to deal with us as partakers of or identified with this law-fulfilling if we will but agree to give up all personal claims to his favor, and accept the claims of him who has magnified the law and made it honorable.

---

made guilty of Adam's sin, which is not inherent in us, but only imputed to us; so are we made righteous by the righteousness of Christ, which is not inherent in us, but only imputed to us" (John Owen).

The legal or *judicial gift* of benefits is certainly different from the *personal meriting* of them; but the benefits are not less real, nor their possession less sure. That they should come to us in a righteous way with the consent and sanction of law is the great thing. The *reality* is to be measured by the actual possession and enjoyment of the benefits and not by the way in which they come. The *security* for them lies in this, that they reach us in a legal and honorable way.

6

THE RIGHTEOUSNESS OF GOD RECKONED TO US

This "everlasting righteousness" comes to us through believing. We are "justified by faith" (Romans 5:1), the fruit of which is "peace with God through our Lord Jesus Christ."

It is of this "everlasting righteousness" that the Apostle Peter speaks when he begins his second epistle thus: "Simon Peter, a servant and an apostle of Jesus Christ, to them that have obtained like precious faith with us, through the righteousness of God and our Savior Jesus Christ"* (2 Peter 1:1).

This righteousness is "reckoned" or "imputed" to all who believe, so that they are treated by God as if it were actually theirs. They are entitled to claim all that which such a righteousness can merit from God as the Judge of righteous claims. It does not become ours gradually, or in fragments or drops; but is transferred to us all at once. It is not that so much of it is reckoned to us (so much to account, as men in business say) in proportion to the strength of our faith, or the warmth of our love, or the fervor of our prayers; but the whole of it passes over to us by *imputation:* We are "accepted in the Beloved" (Ephesians 1:6); we are "complete in him, who is the head of all principality and power" (Colossians 2:10). In its whole quality and quantity it is transferred to us. Its perfection represents us before God; its preciousness, with all that that preciousness can purchase for us, henceforth belongs to us* (1 Peter 1:7).

---

*"To them that have obtained like precious faith with us," *i.e.* with us Jews, who have believed now, and with all our fathers of the past ages, "through [or more properly *in*] the righteousness of him who is our God and Savior." Thus that which is elsewhere called "the righteousness of God" is here called "the righteousness of our God and Savior," *i.e.* of Christ. So that "the righteousness of Christ" is a scriptural expression.

45

The stone, the chief corner-stone, elect and precious—this stone in all its preciousness is ours, not only for resting on, not only for acceptance, but for whatever its divine value can purchase for us. Possessed of this preciousness (imputed, but still *ours*), we go into the heavenly market and buy what we need without stint or end. We get everything upon the credit of his name, because not only has our unworthiness ceased to be recognized by God in his dealings with us, but our demerit has been supplanted by the merit of one who is absolutely and divinely perfect. In his name we carry on all our transactions with God and obtain all that we need by simply using it as our plea. The things that he did not do were laid to his charge, and he was treated as if he had done them all; the things that he did do are put to our account, and we are treated by God as if we had done them all.

This is the scriptural meaning of reckoning or imputing, both in the Old Testament and the New. Let us look at a few of these passages:

Genesis 15:6: "It was *imputed* to him for righteousness"; *i.e.* it was so reckoned to him, that in virtue of it he was treated as being what he was not.

Genesis 31:15: "Are we not *counted* of him strangers?" Are we not treated by him as if we were strangers, not children?

Leviticus 7:18: "Neither shall it be *imputed* unto him that offers it." The excellence of the peace offering shall not be counted to him.

Numbers 18:27: "Your heave-offering shall be *reckoned unto you* as though it were the corn of the threshing-floor." It shall be accepted by God as if it were the whole harvest, and you shall be treated by him accordingly.

---

*In the high priest's breastplate were twelve precious stones on which the names of the twelve tribes were written. The names thus graven shone with all the glory of the gems which contained them. Thus are our names written on the breastplate of the greater High Priest, not only for remembrance, but for glory. They are enveloped in his glory and shine as if all that glory were their own. The lustre of the sardius, the topaz, and the diamond, chased in gold, took away that which was dark and earthly about the name or the person or the tribe. Similarly, the more resplendent lustre of the heavenly gems which glitter in the breastplate of the great Intercessor not only hides all that is unlustrous in us, but gives to us a beauty such as belongs only to him.

2 Samuel 19:19: "Let not my lord *impute* iniquity unto me, neither remember that which your servant did perversely." Do not deal with me according to my iniquity.

Psalm 32:2: "Blessed is the man unto whom the Lord *imputes* not iniquity"; to whom God does not *reckon* his iniquities, but treats him as if they were not (see also Psalm 106:31).

Romans 4:3: "It was *counted* to him for righteousness."

Romans 4:5: "His faith is *counted* for righteousness"; *i.e.*, not as the righteousness, or as the substitute for it, but as bringing him into righteousness (εἰς δικαιοσύνην).

Romans 4:6: "Unto whom God *imputes* righteousness without works."

Romans 4:8: "Blessed is the man to whom the Lord will *not impute* sin."

Romans 4:11: "That righteousness might be *imputed* to them also."

Romans 4:24: "To whom it shall be *imputed,* if we believe on him who raised up Jesus our Lord from the dead."

2 Corinthians 5:19: "Not *imputing* their trespasses unto them."

Galatians 3:6: "It was *accounted* to him for righteousness."

Thus the idea of reckoning to one what does not belong to him and treating him as if he really possessed all that is reckoned to him comes out very clearly.* This is God's way of lifting man out of the horrible pit and the miry clay, of giving him a standing and a privilege and a hope far beyond that which mere pardon gives and no less far above that which the first Adam lost. To be righteous according to the righteousness of the first Adam would have been much; but to be righteous according to the righteousness of the last Adam, the Lord from Heaven, is unspeakably and inconceivably more.

"It is God that justifies," and he does so by imputing to us a righteousness which warrants him as the Judge to justify the unrighteous freely.

It is not simply *because* of this righteousness that Jehovah justifies; but he *legally transfers* it to us so that we can use it, plead it,

---

*See the Greek of Isaiah 53:3, 4. "He was despised, and we *esteemed* him not"; *i.e.* refused to *reckon* him to be what he was. "We did *esteem* him stricken, smitten of God"; we *reckoned* him to be under the curse of God. The word in these two sentences is the same as is elsewhere rendered "imputed."

and appear before God in it, just as if it were wholly our own. Romanists and Socinians have set themselves strongly against the doctrine of "imputed righteousness." But there it stands, written clearly and legibly in the divine word. There it stands, an essential part of the great Bible truth concerning sacrifice and substitution and suretyship. It is as deeply written in the book of Leviticus as in the Epistle to the Romans. It spreads itself over all Scripture and rises gloriously into view in the cross of our Lord Jesus Christ where the "obedience unto death" which makes up this righteousness was completed.* There he, who as our substitute took flesh and was born at Bethlehem, who as our substitute passed through Earth as a man of sorrows and acquainted with grief, consummated his substitution and brought in the "everlasting righteousness." This is the righteousness of which the apostle spoke when he reasoned that, "as by the *disobedience of one* many were made sinners, so by the *obedience of one* shall many be made righteous" (Romans 5:19); when he proclaimed his abnegation of all other righteousnesses: "and be found in him, not having my own righteousness, which is of the law, but that which is by the faith of Christ, even the righteousness which is of God by faith" (Philippians 3:9). This is "the gift of righteousness" regarding which he says: "If by one man's offence death reigned by one; much more they which receive abundance of grace, and of the gift of righteousness, shall reign in life by one, Jesus Christ" (Romans 5:17). The one man's offence rests upon all men "to condemnation" (Romans 5:18); so the one Man's righteousness, as the counteraction or removal of this condemnation, is avail-

---

*"Justifying righteousness is the doing and suffering of Christ when he was in the world. This is clear, because we are said to be justified by his obedience—his obedience to the law (Romans 5:19, 10:4). This righteousness resides in and with the person of Christ; it is of a justifying virtue only by imputation, *i.e.* by God's reckoning it to us, even as our sins made the Lord Jesus a sinner, nay sin, *i.e.* by God's reckoning it to him. The righteousness of God, *i.e.* a righteousness of God's completing, a righteousness of God's bestowing, a righteousness that God gives unto and puts upon all them that believe—a righteousness that stands in the works of Christ, and that is imputed both by the grace and justice of God. The righteousness by which we stand just before God, from the curse, was performed long ago by the person of Christ."
—John Bunyan, *Sermon on Justification by Imputed Righteousness.*

able and efficacious "unto justification of life." The imputation of the first Adam's sin to us, and of the last Adam's righteousness, are thus placed side by side. The transference of our guilt to the Divine Substitute, and the transference of that Substitute's righteousness or perfection to us, must stand or fall together.

This righteousness of God was no common righteousness. It was the righteousness of him who was both God and man; therefore it was not only the righteousness of God, but in addition to this, it was the righteousness of man. It embodied and exhibited all un-created and all created perfection. Never had the like been seen or heard of in Heaven or on Earth before. It was the two-fold perfection of Creaturehood and Creatorship in one resplendent center, one glorious person. The dignity of that person gave a perfection, a vastness, a length and breadth, a height and depth, to that righteous-ness which never had been equalled and which never shall be equal-led forever. It is the perfection of perfection, the excellency of excellency, the holiness of holiness. It is that in which God pre-eminently delights. Never had his law been so kept and honored before. Son of God and Son of man in one person, he in this twofold character keeps the Father's law and in keeping it provides a right-eousness so large and full that it can be shared with others, trans-ferred to others, imputed to others; and God be glorified (as well as the sinner saved) by the transference and imputation. Never had God been so loved as now, with all divine love and with all human love. Never had God been so served and obeyed, as now he has been by him who is "God manifest in flesh." Never had God found one before who for love to the holy law was willing to become its victim that it might be honored; who for love to God was willing not only to be made under the law, but by thus coming under it, to subject himself to death, even the death of the cross; who for love to the fallen creature was willing to take the sinner's place, bear the sin-ner's burden, undergo the sinner's penalty, to assume the sinner's curse, die the sinner's death of shame and anguish, and go down in darkness to the sinner's grave.

The objections against *imputation* all resolve themselves into objections against *substitution* in any form. Vicarious suffering is even more *unreasonable* to some than vicarious obedience, and the arguments used in assailing the former apply with greater force against the latter. Yet human law recognizes both; the "laws of nature" show the existence of both; and the divine law, as interpreted by the great Lawgiver himself, acknowledges both. Man is willing to act on the principle of substitution or representation by another in earthly transactions—such as the payment of debt or the performance of duty or the descent of property; but he is not so willing to admit it, or proceed upon it, in the great transaction between him and God as to condemnation and righteousness. That to which he objects not in temporal things—giving one man the benefit of another's doings or another's sufferings; treating the man who has not paid the debt as if he had done so because another has paid it for him; or recognizing the legal right of a man to large wealth or a vast estate, no part of which he had earned or deserved, but which had come to him as the gift and fruit of another's lifetime's toil—he repudiates in spiritual things as unjust and unreasonable.

Men do not object to receive any kind or amount of this world's goods from another, though they have done nothing to deserve them and everything to make them unworthy of them, but they refuse to accept the favor of God, and a standing in righteousness before him on the ground of what a substitute has done and suffered. In earthly things they are willing to be represented by another, but not in heavenly things. The former is all fair, and just, and legal: the latter is absurd, an insult to their understanding, and a depreciation of their worth! Yet if they prized the heavenly as much as they do the earthly blessing, they would not entertain such scruples nor raise such objections as to receiving it from another as the result of his work. If God is willing that Christ should *represent* us, who are we that we should refuse to be represented by him? If God is willing to deal with us on the footing of Christ's obedience and to reckon that obedience to us as if it had been our own, who are we that we should reject such a method of blessing and call it unjust and impossible? This principle or theory of representation, of one man being treated far beyond his deserts in virtue of his being legally entitled to use the name or claims of another, runs through all earthly transactions. Why should it not in like manner pervade the heavenly?

Rejection of "imputed righteousness" because the words do not actually occur in Scripture is foolish and weak. Such terms as *Christianity*, the *Trinity*, the *Eucharist*, and *Plenary Inspiration* are not to be found in the Bible; yet, inasmuch as the thing, or object, or truth which these words truly and accurately cover is there, the term is received as substantially accurate and made use of without scruple. Such an objection savors more of little-minded cavilling than of the truth-seeking simplicity of faith.*

Refusal to accept the divine "theory" or doctrine of representation in and by another indicates in many cases mere indifference to the blessing to be received; in others, resentment of the way in which that doctrine utterly sets aside all excellency or merit on our part. Men will win the kingdom for themselves; they will deserve eternal life; they will not take forgiveness or righteousness freely from another's hands or be indebted to a substitute for what they are persuaded they can earn by their personal doings. Because the plan of representation or substitution is distasteful and humbling, they call it absurd and unjust. They refuse a heavenly inheritance on such terms, while perhaps at the very moment they are accepting an earthly estate on terms as totally irrespective of their own labor or goodness.

---

*Thus old Anthony Burgess, in 1655, wrote regarding imputation: "The righteousness the believer hath is imputed. It is an *accounted* or *reckoned* righteousness to him; it is not that which he hath inherently in himself, but God through Christ doth esteem of him as if he had it, and so deals with him as wholly righteous. This is a passive, not an active righteousness—a righteousness we *receive*, not that we *do*. This doctrine of imputed righteousness is by all erroneous persons judged to be like the abomination of desolation. Howsoever heretical persons contradict one another in other things, yet against this they are unanimously conspiring. It is well enough known what reproaches and mocks are put upon it by the Popish party, calling it the putative and chimerical righteousness. The Socinians abominate it. The Castellians flout at it, saying they have an imputed learning and imputed modesty that hold imputed righteousness. The Arminians, though they grant faith to be accounted for righteousness, yet think it an idol of the Protestants' brain to say that Christ's righteousness is imputed to us, and say that it is nowhere expressed in Scripture. . . . Let this satisfy us, that the Scripture doth often mention an imputed righteousness, and therefore that it should not be matter of reproach, but worthy of all acceptation; and certainly, seeing none of us has such an inherent righteousness within ourselves as is able to endure before so perfect and holy a God, we ought greatly to rejoice in the goodness and mercy of God, who had provided such glorious robes for us, that when we were wholly naked and undone, hath procured a righteousness for us that neither men nor angels could bring about."

The Judge must either be the justifier or the condemner. That Judge is Jehovah. It is his office to condemn; it is his office also to justify. He does not condemn by *infusing* sin into the person who appears before him; so he does not justify by *infusing* righteousness into the sinner whom he acquits. It is as *Judge* that he acquits. But he does not merely acquit or absolve. He goes beyond this. The marvelous way in which he has met the claims of justice so as to enable him to pronounce a righteous *acquittal* enables him to replace, either on his own former place of innocence or on a higher, the sinner whom he absolves so freely and so completely. It was by representation or substitution of the just for the unjust that he was enabled to acquit, and it is by the same representation or substitution that he lifts into a more glorious position the acquitted man.

The representative or substitute being the Son of God and therefore of infinite dignity in his person, the excellency of that which he is and does, when conveyed or reckoned to another, gives that other a claim to be treated far higher than he could otherwise in any circumstances have possessed. Some may have expressed his transference in terms too strong and absolute, as if we actually became as righteous as he is, as near to God as he is, as infinitely the objects of the Father's love as he is. But though there may have been unwise utterances on this point, which have needlessly afforded cause of offence and objection, it remains true that the man who believes in Jesus Christ—from the moment that he so believes—not only receives divine absolution from all guilt, but is so made legally possessor of his infinite righteousness that all to which that righteousness entitles becomes his, and he is henceforth treated by God according to the perfection of the perfect one, as if that perfection had been his own. "As he is, so are we [even] in *this world*" (1 John 4:17), that is, even *now*, in our state of imperfection, though men of unclean lips, and though dwelling among a people of unclean lips. As it is elsewhere written, "There is therefore *now* no condemnation to them that are in Christ Jesus" (Romans 8:1). Not only are we "delivered from the wrath to come" (1 Thessalonians 1:10), not only shall we "not come into condemnation" (John 5:24), not only are we "justified from all things" (Acts 13:39), but we are "made* *the righteousness of God* in him" (2 Corinthians 5:21).

---

*Literally, we "become"—γινωμεθα.

The transaction is not one of *borrowing.* The perfection made over to us is *given,* not *lent,* by God. It becomes ours *in law,* ours for all legal ends, ours as efficaciously as if it had been from first to last our own in very deed.

The transaction is a real one between the sinner and God and carries with it all legal consequences, just as if the sinner had personally discharged his own debts and obtained a judicial *absolvitor* from all further claims whatever, a receipt in full from him to whom the great debt was due.

The transaction is one to which all the parties concerned have consented as being fully satisfied that injury has been done to none; nay, that all have been greatly more benefited by this mode of settlement than by the more direct one of the parties punishable undergoing the punishment in their own persons. When thus not merely no injustice is done to anyone, but when *more than justice* is done to all; when no one is defrauded, but when each *gets far more than his due;* how foolish, how preposterous, to speak of imputation as a violation of law and a subversion of the principles of righteous government!

The transaction is not one of indifference to sin or obliterative of the distinction between righteousness and unrighteousness. It is one which, of all that can be imagined, is most fitted to show *the evil of evil,* the malignity of sin, the divine hatred of all departure from perfection, the regard which God has to his law, his awful appreciation of justice, and his determination to secure at any cost— even the death of his Son—the righteous foundations of the universe and the sanctities of his eternal throne.

If the Christ of God, in his sorrowful life below, be but a specimen of suffering humanity or a model of patient calmness under wrong, not one of these things is manifested or secured. He is but one fragment more of a confused and disordered world where everything has broken loose from its anchorage, and each is dashing against the other in unmanageable chaos without any prospect of a holy or tranquil issue. He is an example of the complete triumph of evil over goodness, of wrong over right, of Satan over God—one from whose history we can draw only this terrific conclusion: God has lost the control of his own world; sin has become too great a power for God either to regulate or extirpate; the utmost that God can do is to produce a rare example of suffering holiness which he allows the world to tread upon without being able effectually to interfere; righteousness, after ages of buffeting and scorn, must retire from the field in utter helplessness and permit the unchecked reign of evil.

If the cross be the mere exhibition of self-sacrifice and patient meekness, then the hope of the world is gone. We had always thought that there was a potent *purpose* of God at work *in connection with the sin-bearing work* of the holy sufferer which, allowing sin for a season to develop itself, was preparing and evolving a power which would utterly overthrow it—and sweep Earth clean of evil—moral and physical. But if the crucified Christ be the mere self-denying man, we have nothing more at work for the overthrow of evil than has again and again been witnessed when some hero or some martyr rose above the level of his age to protest against evils which he could not eradicate and to bear witness in life and death for truth and righteousness—in vain.

The transaction is, in all its aspects and in its bearings on all parties and interests, strictly and nobly *righteous*. It provides a *righteous* channel through which God's free love may flow down to man. It lays a *righteous* foundation for the pardon of sin. It secures a *righteous* welcome for the returning sinner. It makes the justification of the justified even more righteous than his condemnation would have been; while it makes the condemnation of the condemned not only doubly righteous, but at once a vindication and an exhibition of infinite and immutable justice.

There can be no justification without some kind of righteousness, and according to the nature or value of that righteousness will the justification be. That justification will necessarily partake of the value of the righteousness which justifies. If the righteousness be poor and finite, our standing as justified men will be the same. If it be glorious and divine, even such will our standing be. God the justifier, acting according to the excellency of that righteousness and recognizing its claims in behalf of all who consent to be treated according to its value, deals with each believing man—weak as his faith may be—in conformity with the demands of that righteousness. All that it can claim for us we may ask and expect; all that it can claim for us God will assuredly bestow. He by whom, in believing, we consent to be represented puts in the claim for us in *his* name; and the demands of that name are as just as they are irresistible.

Our legal responsibilities as transgressors of the law are transferred to him; and his legal claims, as the fulfiller of the law, pass over to us. It is not a transference of characters nor an exchange of persons that we mean by this; but a transference of liabilities, an exchange of judicial demands. Very strikingly is the case between the sinner and God put in our Lord's parable of the two debtors, of which these words are the sum: "When they had nothing to pay, he frankly forgave them both" (Luke 7:42). Here is our thorough bankruptcy and God's full discharge. What can law say to us after this? "It is God that justifies." We are bankrupts; our assets are nothing; God looks at the case, pities us, and clears everything.

The epithet "fictitious" which some have applied to this representation need not trouble or alarm us. The question with us is not, Can we clear up fully the abstract principles which the transaction embodies? but, Does it *carry with it legal consequences* by which we are set in a new standing before God and entitled to plead, in all our dealings with God, the meritoriousness of an infinitely perfect life the payment effected in behalf of those who had nothing to pay, by an infinitely perfect death?

Thus "grace reigns through righteousness unto eternal life through Jesus Christ our Lord" (Romans 5:21).* God's free love has found for itself a righteous channel along which it flows in all its fulness to the ungodly. For while all that the believing man receives, he receives from *grace;* yet it is no less true that all that he receives, he receives from *righteousness,* from the hand of a righteous God acting according to the claims of a righteousness which is absolutely and divinely perfect.

He who refuses to be represented by another before God must represent himself and draw near to God on the strength of what he is in himself or what he has done. How he is likely to fare in such an approach, let his own conscience tell him if he will not believe the explicit declaration of the Holy Spirit that "through him [Christ] we have access by one Spirit to the Father" (Ephesians 2:18); or Christ's own affirmation concerning this: "I am the way," and "I am the door" (John 10:9, 14:6).

---

*"Through (διά) righteousness," and also "through (διά) Jesus Christ our Lord"; the one the active instrument, the other the efficient cause: (1) God the justifier, (2) Christ the cause, (3) righteousness the instrument.

As for him who, conscious of unfitness to draw near to God by reason of personal imperfection, is willing to be represented by the Son of God and to substitute a divine claim and merit for a human; let him know that God is willing to receive him with all his imperfection because of the perfection of another, legally transferred to him by the just God and Judge; that God is presenting to him a righteousness not only sufficient to clear him from all guilt and to pay his penalty to the full, but to exalt him to a new rank and dignity such as he could not possibly acquire by the labors or prayers or goodnesses of ten thousand such lives as his own.

"Christ is all and in all" (Colossians 3:11). He who knows this, knows what fully satisfies and cheers. He who knows this best has the deepest and truest peace: He has learned the secret of being always a sinner, yet always righteous; always incomplete, yet always complete; always empty, yet always full; always poor, yet always rich. We would not say of that fulness, Drink deep or taste not; for even to taste is to be blest. But yet we say, Drink deep; for he who drinks deepest is the happiest as well as the holiest man.*

Recognition of the *perfection* of the Lord Jesus Christ, as to personal excellency, official suitableness, and vicarious value, is that only which satisfies the *heart* and *conscience* of the sinner. It satisfies the former by presenting it with the most lovable of all lovable objects on which a heart can rest, and the latter by furnishing it with that which can alone remove from the trembling conscience

---

*"Think not that to live always on Christ for justification is a low and beggarly thing—a staying at the foundation. For, let me tell you, depart from a sense of the meritorious means of your justification before God, and you will quickly grow light, and frothy, and vain; you will be subject to errors and delusions, for this is not to 'hold the head,' from which nourishment is administered. Why not live upon Christ alway; and especially as he standeth the Mediator between God and the soul, defending thee with the merit of his blood, and covering thee with His infinite righteousness from the wrath of God and the curse of the law? Can there be any greater comfort ministered to thee, than to know that thy person stands just before God; just, and justified from all things that would otherwise swallow thee up? Is peace with God and assurance of heaven of so little respect with thee, that thou slightest the very foundation thereof, even faith in the blood and righteousness of Christ?"
—John Bunyan, *Justification by Imputed Righteousness.*

every possible ground for claim. True knowledge of the person of him who is "the Christ of God," appreciation of his completed sacrifice and living attachment to himself, can alone meet the evil condition into which man has sunk; not only lifting him out of the horrible pit and out of the miry clay; not only setting his feet upon the eternal rock; but raising him up into a region of peace and holiness such as no less costly means could have accomplished for the fallen son of Adam.

"He who knew no sin was made sin for us." On this basis we build for eternity. The assumption of all our legal responsibilities by a divine substitute is that which brings us deliverance. These responsibilities were great, and no effort of ours to rid ourselves of them could possibly succeed. They must all be fully met. Such judicial claims as are brought against the sinner cannot be waived. They are righteous claims and must be settled righteously. God offers to settle them for us by transferring them to one who can be answerable for them. The basis of this eternal settlement was laid at the cross, and on that basis God is willing to deal with any sinner for the complete canceling of all his liabilities.

The second man came, as the Righteous One, to undo by his righteousness all that the first man, as the unrighteous one, had done by his unrighteousness. Yet such is the power of sin that it took thirty-three years of righteousness to undo what one act of unrighteousness had done. One act of disobedience to one statute had done the evil; a lifetime's obedience to the whole law of God is required for the undoing. Only by this can man be replaced in that condition of righteousness in which God can accept him and the law recognize him as entitled to blessing.

---

*"Labor therefore diligently, that not only out of the time of temptation, but also in the danger and conflict of death, when your conscience is thoroughly afraid with the remembrance of your sins past, and the devil assaults you with great violence, going about to overwhelm you with heaps, floods, and whole seas of sins, to terrify you, to draw you from Christ, and to drive you to despair; that then, I say, you may be able to say with sure confidence, Christ the Son of God was given, not for the righteous and holy, but for the unrighteous and sinners. If I were righteous and had no sin, I should have no need of Christ to be my reconciler. Why then, O you peevish "holy" Satan, will you make me to be holy, and to seek righteousness in myself, when in very deed I have

Our *characters* are not transferred to Christ, but our *liabilities* are; and in our acceptance of God's mode of transference, we make the complete exchange by which we are absolved from all guilt and enter into a state of "no condemnation." Sin reckoned to Christ as our substitute, and righteousness reckoned to us as the acceptors of that substitute: this is deliverance, and peace, and life eternal.*

---

nothing in me but sins, and most grievous sins? Not feigned or trifling sins, but such as are against the first table; to wit, great infidelity, doubting, despair, contempt of God, hatred, ignorance, and blaspheming of God, unthankfulness, abusing of God's name, neglecting, loathing, and despising the word of God, and such like."

—Martin Luther

7

NOT FAITH, BUT CHRIST

Our justification is the direct result of our believing the Gospel; our knowledge of our own justification comes from our believing God's promise of justification to everyone who believes these glad tidings. For there is not only the divine testimony, but there is the promise annexed to it, assuring eternal life to every one who receives that testimony. There is first, then, a believed *Gospel,* and then there is a believed *promise.* The latter is the "appropriation," as it is called; which, after all, is nothing but the acceptance of the *promise* which is everywhere coupled with the Gospel message. The believed Gospel *saves,* but it is the believed promise that *assures* us of this salvation.

Yet, after all, faith is not our righteousness. It is accounted to us *in order to (εἰς)* righteousness (Romans 4:5), but not *as* righteousness; for in that case it would be a *work* like any other doing of man. As such, it would be incompatible with the righteousness of the Son of God; the "righteousness which is by faith." Faith connects us with the righteousness and is therefore totally distinct from it. To confound the one with the other is to subvert the whole Gospel of the grace of God. Our act of faith must ever be a separate thing from that which we believe.

God reckons the believing man as having done *all righteousness,* though he has not done *any* and though his faith is not righteousness. In this sense it is that faith is counted to us for, or in order to, righteousness; and that we are "justified by faith." Faith does not justify as a work, or as a moral act, or a piece of goodness, or as a gift of the Spirit; but simply because it is the bond between us and the substitute—a very slender bond in one sense, but strong as iron in another. The work of Christ *for us* is the object of faith; the Spirit's work *in us* is that which produces this faith: It is out of the former, not out of the latter, that our peace and justification come.

Without the touch of the rod the water would not have gushed forth; yet it was the *rock,* and not the *rod,* that contained the water. The bringer of the sacrifice into the tabernacle was to lay his hand upon the head of the sheep or the bullock. Otherwise the offering would not have been accepted for him. But the laying on of his hand was not the same as the victim on which it was laid. The serpent-bitten Israelite was to look at the uplifted serpent of brass in order to be healed. But his looking was not the brazen serpent. We may say it was his looking that healed him, just as the Lord said, "Your faith has saved you"; but this is figurative language. It was not his act of looking that healed him, but the object to which he looked. So faith is not our righteousness. It merely knits us to the righteous one and makes us partakers of his righteousness. By a natural figure of speech, faith is often magnified into something great; whereas it is really nothing but our consenting to be saved by another. Its supposed magnitude is derived from the greatness of the object which it grasps, the excellence of the righteousness which it accepts. Its preciousness is not its own, but the preciousness of him to whom it links us.

Faith is not our physician; it only brings us to the Physician. It is not even our medicine; it only administers the medicine, divinely prepared by him who "heals all our diseases." In all our believing, let us remember God's words to Israel: "I am Jehovah, who heals you" (Exodus 15:26). Our faith is but our touching Jesus; and what is even this, in reality, but *his touching us?*

Faith is not our savior. It was not faith that was born at Bethlehem and died on Golgotha for us. It was not faith that loved us and gave itself for us, that bore our sins in its own body on the tree, that died and rose again for our sins. Faith is one thing, and the Savior is another. Faith is one thing, and the cross is another. Let us not confound them nor ascribe to a poor, imperfect act of man that which belongs exclusively to the Son of the living God.

Faith is not perfection. Yet only by perfection—either our own or another's—can we be saved. That which is imperfect cannot justify, and an imperfect faith could not in any sense be a righteousness. If it is to justify, it must be perfect. It must be like "the Lamb, without blemish and without spot." An imperfect faith may connect us with the perfection of another; but it cannot of itself do anything for us, either in protecting us from wrath or securing the divine acquittal. All faith here is imperfect. Our security is this: It matters not how poor or weak our faith may be; if it touches the perfect one, all is well. The touch draws out the virtue that is in him, and we are saved. The slightest imperfection in our faith, if faith were our righteousness, would be fatal to every hope. But the imperfection of our faith, however great, if faith be but the approximation or contact between us and the fulness of the substitute, is no hindrance to our participation in his righteousness. God has asked and provided a perfect righteousness; he nowhere asks nor expects a perfect faith. An earthenware pitcher can convey water to the traveler's thirsty lips as well as one of gold; nay, a broken vessel even, if there be but "a shard to take water from the pit" (Isaiah 30:14) will suffice. So a feeble, very feeble faith will connect us with the righteousness of the Son of God—the faith, perhaps, that can only cry, "Lord, I believe; help my unbelief."

Faith is not *satisfaction to God*. In no sense and in no aspect can faith be said to satisfy God or to satisfy the law. Yet if it is to be our righteousness, it must satisfy. Being *imperfect,* it cannot satisfy; being merely human, it cannot satisfy even though it were perfect. That which satisfies must be capable of bearing our guilt; and that which bears our guilt must be not only perfect, but divine. It is a sin bearer that we need, and our faith cannot be a sin bearer. Faith can expiate no guilt, can accomplish no propitiation, can pay no penalty, can wash away no stain, can provide no righteousness. It brings us to the cross, where there is expiation and propitiation, and payment, and cleansing, and righteousness; but in itself it has no merit and no virtue.

Faith is not Christ, nor the cross of Christ. Faith is not the blood, nor the sacrifice. It is not the altar, nor the laver, nor the mercy-seat, nor the incense. It does not work, but accepts a work done ages ago; it does not wash, but leads us to the fountain opened for sin and for uncleanness. It does not create; it merely links us to that new thing which was created when the "everlasting righteousness" was brought in (Daniel 9:24).

And as faith goes on, so it continues; always the beggar's outstretched hand, never the rich man's gold; always the cable, never the anchor; the knocker, not the door, or the palace, or the table; the handmaid, not the mistress; the lattice which lets in the light, not the sun.

Without worthiness in itself, it knits us to the infinite worthiness of him in whom the Father delights; and so knitting us, it presents us perfect in the perfection of another. Though it is not the foundation laid in Zion, it brings us to that foundation and keeps us there, "grounded and settled" (Colossians 1:23), that we may not be moved away from the hope of the Gospel. Though it is not "the Gospel," the "glad tidings," it receives the good news as God's eternal verities and bids the soul rejoice in them; though it is not the burnt offering, it stands still and gazes on the ascending flame which assures us that the wrath which should have consumed the sinner has fallen upon the substitute.

Though faith is not "the righteousness," it is the tie between it and us. It realizes our present standing before God in the excellency of his own Son, and it tells us that our eternal standing in the ages to come is in the same excellency and depends on the perpetuity of that righteousness which can never change. For never shall we *put off* that Christ whom we *put on* when we believed (Romans 13:14; Galatians 3:27). This divine raiment is "to everlasting." It grows not old, it cannot be torn, and its beauty fades not away.

Nor does faith lead us away from that cross to which at first it led us. Some in our day speak as if we soon get beyond the cross and might leave it behind; that the cross having done all it could do for us when first we came under its shadow, we may quit it and go forward; that to remain always at the cross is to be babes, not men.

But what is the cross? It is not the mere wooden pole, or some imitation of it, such as Romanists use. These we may safely leave behind us. We need not pitch our tent upon the literal Golgotha or in Joseph's garden. But the great truth which the cross represents we can no more part with than we can part with life eternal. In this sense, to turn our back upon the cross is to turn our back upon Christ crucified—to give up our connection with the Lamb that was slain. The truth is that all that Christ did and suffered—from the manger to the tomb—forms one glorious whole, no part of which shall ever become needless or obsolete and no part of which we can ever leave without forsaking the whole. I am always at the manger, and yet I know that mere incarnation cannot save; always in Gethsemane, and yet I believe that its agony was not the finished work; always at the cross with my face toward it and my eye on the crucified one, and yet I am persuaded that the sacrifice there was completed once for all; always looking into the grave, though I rejoice that it is empty, and that "he is not here, but is risen"; always resting (with the angel) on the stone that was rolled away, and handling the graveclothes, and realizing a risen Christ, an ascended and interceding Lord: yet on no pretext whatever leaving any part of my Lord's life or death behind me, but unceasingly keeping up my connection with him, as born, living, dying, buried, and rising again, and drawing out from each part some new blessing every day and hour.

Man, in his natural spirit of self-justifying legalism, has tried to get away from the cross of Christ and its perfection, or to erect another cross instead, or to set up a screen of ornaments between himself and it, or to alter its true meaning into something more congenial to his tastes, or to transfer the virtue of it to some act or performance or feeling of his own. Thus the simplicity of the cross is nullified and its saving power denied.

The cross saves completely, or not at all. Our faith does not divide the work of salvation between itself and the cross. It is the acknowledgment that the cross alone saves, and that it saves alone. Faith adds nothing to the cross or to its healing virtue. It owns the fulness, and sufficiency, and suitableness of the work done there and bids the toiling spirit cease from its labors and enter into rest. Faith does not come to Calvary to *do* anything. It comes to see the glorious spectacle of all things done and to accept this completion without a misgiving as to its efficacy. It listens to the "It is finished!" of the sin bearer and says, "Amen." Where faith begins, there labor ends—labor, I mean, *for* life and pardon. Faith is rest, not toil. It is the giving up of all the former weary efforts to do or feel something good in order to induce God to love and pardon; the calm reception of the truth so long rejected that God is not waiting for any such inducements, but loves and pardons of his own goodwill and is showing that goodwill to any sinner who will come to him on such a footing, casting away his own poor performances or goodnesses and relying implicitly upon the free love of him who so loved the world that he gave his only begotten Son.

Faith is the acknowledgment of the entire absence of all goodness in us and the recognition of the cross as the substitute for all the want on our part. Faith saves because it owns the complete salvation of another, not because it contributes anything to that salvation.

There is no dividing or sharing the work between our own belief and him in whom we believe. The whole work is his, not ours, from first to last. Faith does not believe in itself, but in the Son of God. Like the beggar, it receives everything, but gives nothing. It consents to be a debtor forever to the free love of God. Its resting place is the foundation laid in Zion. It rejoices in another, not in itself. Its song is, "Not by works of righteousness which we have done, but by his mercy he saved us."

Christ crucified is to be the burden of our preaching, and the substance of our belief, from first to last. At no time in the saint's life does he cease to need the cross, though at times he may feel that his special need (in spiritual perplexity or the exigency of conflict with evil) may be the incarnation, or the agony in the garden, or the resurrection, or the hope of the promised advent, to be glorified in his saints, and admired in all them that believe.

But the question is not, What truths are we to believe? but, What truths are we to believe *for justification?*

That Christ is to come again in glory and in majesty, as Judge and King, is an article of the Christian faith, the disbelief of which would almost lead us to doubt the Christianity of him who disbelieves it. Yet we are not in any sense justified by the second advent of our Lord, but solely by his first. We believe in his ascension, yet our justification is not connected with it. So we believe his resurrection, yet are we not justified by faith in it, but by faith in his death—that death which made him at once our propitiation and our righteousness.

"He was raised again on account of our having been justified" (Romans 4:25) is the clear statement of the word. The resurrection was the visible pledge of a justification already accomplished.

"The power of his resurrection" (Philippians 3:10) does not refer to atonement, or pardon, or reconciliation; but to our being renewed in the spirit of our minds, to our being "begotten again unto a living hope, by the resurrection from the dead" (1 Peter 1:3). That which is *internal,* such as our quickening, our strengthening, our renewing, may be connected with resurrection and resurrection power; but that which is *external,* such as God's pardoning, and justifying, and accepting, must be connected with the cross alone.

The doctrine of our being justified by an *infused resurrection* *righteousness,* or, as it is called, justification in a risen Christ,* is a clean subversion of the surety's work when "he died for our sins, according to the Scriptures," or when "he washed us from our sins in his own blood," or when he gave us the robes "washed white in the blood of the Lamb."

It is *the blood* that justifies (Romans 5:9). It is the blood that pacifies the conscience, purging it from dead works to serve the living God (Hebrews 9:14). It is *the blood* that emboldens us to enter through the veil into the holiest and go up to the sprinkled mercy-seat. It is *the blood* that we are to drink for the quenching of our thirst (John 6:55). It is *the blood* by which we have peace with God (Colossians 1:20). It is *the blood* through which we have redemption (Ephesians 1:7), by which we are brought nigh (Ephesians 2:13), by which we are sanctified (Hebrews 13:12). It is the *blood* which is the seal of the everlasting covenant (Hebrews 13:20). It is the *blood* which cleanses (1 John 1:7), which gives us victory (Revelation 12:11), and with which we have communion in the Supper of the Lord (1 Corinthians 10:16). It is the *blood* which is the purchase money or ransom of the church of God (Acts 20:28).

The blood and the resurrection are very different things; for the blood is death, and the resurrection is life.

It is remarkable that in the book of Leviticus there is no reference to resurrection in any of the sacrifices. It is death throughout. All that is needed for a sinner's pardon, and justification, and cleansing, and peace, is there fully set forth in symbol—and that symbol is death upon the altar. Justification by any kind of infused or inherent righteousness is wholly inconsistent with the services of the tabernacle, most of all justification by an infused resurrection-righteousness.

The sacrifices are God's symbolical exposition of the way of a sinner's approach and acceptance, and in none of these does resurrection hold any place. If justification be in a *risen* Christ, then

---

*Mr. Edward Irving, Dr. John Henry Newman, and the followers of Mr. John Nelson Darby are the modern upholders of this new form of old heresy. Formerly it was simply justification by an infused righteousness, now it is by an infused righteousness derived from Christ's resurrection. See Dr. Newman's sermon, *Christ's Resurrection the Source of Justification.*

assuredly that way was not revealed to Israel; and the manifold offerings, so minutely detailed, did not answer the question, How may man be just with God? nor give to the worshippers of old one hint as to the way by which God was to justify the ungodly.

"Christ in us, the hope of glory" (Colossians 1:27) is a well-known and blessed truth; but Christ in us, *our justification*, is a ruinous error, leading men away from a crucified Christ—a Christ crucified *for us*. Christ *for us* is one truth; Christ *in us* is quite another. The mingling of these two together, or the transposition of them, is the nullifying of the one finished work of the substitute. Let it be granted that Christ in us is the source of holiness and fruitfulness (John 15:4); but let it never be overlooked that first of all there must be Christ *for us* as our propitiation, our justification, our righteousness. The *risen Christ in us*, our justification, is a modern theory which subverts the cross. Washing, pardoning, reconciling, justifying, all come from the one work of the cross, not from resurrection. The dying Christ completed the work for us from which all the above benefits flow. The risen Christ but sealed and applied what, three days before, he had done once for all.

It is somewhat remarkable that in the Lord's Supper (as in the Passover) there is no reference to resurrection. The broken body and the shed blood are the Alpha and Omega of that ordinance. In it we have communion (not with Christ as risen and glorified, but) with the body of Christ and the blood of Christ (1 Corinthians 10:16), that is, Christ *upon the cross*. "This do in remembrance of me." "As often as you eat this bread, and drink this cup, you show the *Lord's death* till he come." If, after we have been at the cross, we are to pass on and leave it behind us as no longer needed, seeing we are *justified by the risen Christ in us*, let those who hold that deadly error say why all reference to resurrection should be excluded from the great feast and why the *death* of the Lord should be the one object presented to us at the table.

"Life in a risen Christ" is another way of expressing the same error. If by this were meant only that resurrection has been made the channel or instrument through which the life and the justification are secured for us on and by the cross—as when the apostle speaks of our being begotten again unto a lively hope by the "resurrection of Christ from the dead," or when we are said to be "risen with Christ"—one would not object to the phraseology. But when we find it used as expressive of *dissociation of these benefits from the cross and derivation of them from resurrection solely,* then do we condemn it as untrue and antiscriptural. For concerning this "life" let us hear the words of the Lord: "The bread that I will give is *my flesh,* which I will give for *the life* of the world" (John 6:51). "Except you eat *the flesh* of the Son of man and drink *his blood,* you have no life in you. Whoever eats *my flesh* and drinks *my blood has eternal life,* and I will raise him up at the last day. For *my flesh* is meat indeed, and *my blood* is drink indeed. He that eats *my flesh,* and drinks *my blood,* dwells in me, and I in him" (John 6:53–56).

This assuredly is not the doctrine of "life in a risen Christ," or "a risen Christ in us, our justification and life." I do not enter on the exposition of these verses. I simply cite them. They bear witness to the cross. They point to the broken body and shed blood as our daily and hourly food, our life-long feast from which there comes into us *the life* which the Son of man, by his *death,* has obtained for us. That *flesh* is life imparting; that *blood* is life imparting; and this not once, but forevermore. It is not *incarnation* on the one hand, nor is it *resurrection* on the other, on which we are thus to feed and out of which this life comes forth; it is that which lies between these two—death—the sacrificial death of the Son of God. It is not the personality nor the life history of the Christ of God which is the special quickener and nourishment of our souls, but the blood shedding. Not that we are to separate the former from the latter, but still it is on the latter that we are specially to feed, and this all the days of our lives.

"Christ, our passover, has been sacrificed for us." Here we rest, protected by the paschal blood and feeding on the paschal lamb, with its unleavened bread and bitter herbs, from day to day. "Let us keep the feast" (1 Corinthians 5:8). Wherever we are, let us keep it. For we carry our passover with us, always ready, always fresh. With girded loins and staff in hand, as wayfarers, we move along through the rough or the smooth of the wilderness, our face toward the land of promise.

That paschal lamb is *Christ crucified.* As such he is our protection, our pardon, our righteousness, our food, our strength, our peace. Fellowship with him upon the cross is the secret of a blessed and holy life.

We feed on that which has passed through the fire, on that

which has come from the altar. No other food can quicken or sustain the spiritual life of a believing man. The *unbroken* body will not suffice, nor will the risen or glorified body avail. The broken body and shed blood of the Son of God are the viands on which we feast; and it is under the shadow of the cross that we sit down to partake of these and find refreshment for our daily journey, strength for our hourly warfare. His flesh is meat indeed; his blood is drink indeed.

8

WHAT THE RESURRECTION OF THE SUBSTITUTE HAS DONE

Death is not resurrection, and the benefits of the Surety's death are not the same as those of his resurrection. Yet let us not overlook the "glorious things" spoken concerning the latter.

Our justified life, or our life as justified men, is certainly in one sense resurrection life, produced and sustained by resurrection power. But not for a moment is that justified life severed from the cross, nor is the justified man to lose sight of his indebtedness to the cross for justification.

That we are risen with Christ is the truth of God. Oneness with him who rose is our privilege and our standing. But oneness is not substitution; and it is not by the former, but by the latter, that we are justified. Resurrection points us back to a finished substitution and seals its blessings to us.

"Justified in the Spirit" is one of the apostle's references to Christ's resurrection. As he was brought again from the dead by the blood of the everlasting covenant (Hebrews 13:20), so was he justified in or by the Spirit in raising him from the dead. He died as a criminal and went down to the grave as such; but the Spirit raises him and thereby declares him righteous, free from the imputed guilt under which he went down to the tomb.

But let us look a little more minutely into Christ's resurrection, lest we should be led to undervalue it. The resurrection must not hide the cross; neither must the cross hide the resurrection.

The words of the angel to the women are meant for us: "He is not here, for he is risen" (Matthew 28:6).

Man did all that he could to hinder the resurrection of the Son of God. He had succeeded in slaying the prince of life; and he is resolved that, if he can help it, the dead shall not arise. Samson is in prison, and must be kept there. The great stone, the watch, the Roman seal are all proofs of this determination.

But he knows not his prisoner. He might as well bind the whirlwind with a cord of silk, or shut up the lightning in one of his chambers and say to it, Thou shalt not go forth. Death itself, stronger than man, could not hold its prey. Before the dawn of the third day, the earthquake shook the tomb (the earthquake of Psalm 18:6, 7), the angel of the Lord descended, the stone was rolled away, the seal was broken, and the dead came forth.

Even his own believe not that he will rise. They would not try to hinder his resurrection, but, treating it as a thing incredible, they act as those who believe that all is over and that the cross has destroyed their hopes. They would not close the sepulchre, nor seal it; they would roll away the stone and break the seal, but this is only to anoint him for his final burial. It is not the expression of hope, but of despair.

But the tomb of the Son of God is the place of light, not of darkness; of hope, not of despair; of life, not of death. They come to look on the dead; they find the living. The seekers of the crucified Jesus find the risen Son of God. The garments of death are all that the tomb contains; the linen clothes—still stained with blood—and the carefully folded napkin—folded by angels' hands, if not by his own. They had brought their myrrh and aloes and spices to keep corruption from entering; forgetful that it is the Incorruptible whose body they are thus needlessly though lovingly embalming, ignorant of the meaning of the ancient promise, "You will not allow your Holy One to see corruption."

But friend and enemy are both at fault. The unbelief of the former and the resistance of the latter are met equally with a strange surprise. For God's thoughts are not our thoughts nor his ways our ways. The angel of the Lord descends; he rolls back the stone; he sits upon it to show himself in his brightness to the watchers; he opens the gate that the Holy One may go forth. Not that he raises or assists in raising the Son of God. That is beyond the mightiest of these mighty ones, those angels that excel in strength. But he is honored to have a share in the scene as porter or doorkeeper of that glorious shrine. With him came the earthquake, the second that had occurred during these three days—the first being when the prince of life entered the chambers of death, and at the open door many of the dead saints of other days came forth; the second being when this same prince of life left these chambers and burst the bands of death, shaking creation with the tread of his feet as he marched forth in triumph.

The earthquake and the brightness were too terrible for man to bear. "For fear of him, the keepers did shake and became as dead men." Nor does he try to allay their terror. Let them tremble on. But for those who are seeking the crucified one he has words of love and peace. To the keepers he was as the lightning; to the women he was as the dayspring from on high. "Fear not; I know that you seek Jesus, who was crucified."

That which follows is the angel's message to these women— and to us no less in these last days. It is the reason for the cheer, the comfort he had spoken. It is the blessed contents of the cup, the ingredients of the heavenly wine,which he was giving them to drink. And the substance of it is, "Jesus lives." The comfort with which the Lord himself once comforted the sorrowing father of Capernaum was, "The maid is not dead, but sleeps"; so the comfort ministered by the angel is like this, only it goes far beyond it: "He is not dead; he does not even sleep: He has awakened; he has arisen." And as the Lord calmed the fears of his disciples once with, "Be of good cheer; it is I; be not afraid"; so did the angel here. As in Patmos the Lord allayed the alarm of the beloved disciple with "Fear not, I am the First and the Last; I am he that lives, and was dead; and behold, I am alive forevermore"; so does the angel soothe the fear of the trembling women: "Fear not; he is not here; he is risen: Come, see the place where the Lord lay."

Let us mark, then, the glad tidings which the angel brings us regarding him who died and was buried.

He is not here. This is the only place regarding which it could be accounted good news to say, Christ is *not* here. Christ is *here,* was good news at Bethany, at Jericho, at Nain, at Capernaum, or on the sea of Galilee; but Christ is *not* here is the good news from Joseph's tomb. A *present* Christ would be accounted the joy and security of other places; it is an *absent* Christ that is announced as the blessing, the consolation, here. He is *not* here is one of the gladdest sounds that ever fell on human ears. Were he still here, what and where should *we* have been?

And who is it that you are seeking here? The mortal or the

immortal? And what place is this in which you expect to find the Son of God? In a grave? Is this the place for immortality? Is it likely that there should be life in the dwellings of death? Why seek ye the living among the dead? No; not here—not *here;* not in this place of death can the prince of life be found. He *was* here, indeed; but he *is* not. These rock walls and this rock gate cannot hold him. He *was* in Gethsemane, in Pilate's palace, on the cross; but not now. These he has visited, but in none of them has he remained. He has left them all behind. With him it is all life, and incorruption, and glory now. He is not here!

If not here, *where?* That we soon discover when we follow him to Emmaus and to Galilee. But even though we knew not, does it matter save for this: that we may learn that his disappearance has not been a forsaking of Earth, nor a turning his back upon the children of men? His disappearance from the tomb is only the carrying out of his love.

He is risen. He was laid down upon that rocky floor, but only to rest there for a day. For that tomb was his first earthly resting-place; all before that was weariness. Having rested there for a short season, he rises; and with renewed strength, into which hereafter no element of weariness can enter, he resumes his work. He has not been carried off, either by friend or enemy. He has been raised by the Father as the righteous one; the fulfiller of his purpose; the finisher of his work; the destroyer of death; the conqueror of him who has the power of death; the Father's beloved Son in whom he is well pleased. This true temple has been destroyed, only to be rebuilt in greater and more undecaying magnificence. This true Siloam has only for three days intermitted the flow of its missioned waters, that it might gush forth in larger fulness. This true Sun has only for three days been darkened, that it might be relighted in its incorruptible glory.

He is risen! Yes; and now we see more fully the meaning of his own words spoken at a tomb over one whom death had bound: "I am the resurrection and the life"—himself at once the raiser and the raised, the quickener and the quickened, the possessor and the giver of an infinite life—a higher kind of life than that which the first Adam knew—a life which can force its way into the dungeons of death, transforming them by its resistless power into the dwellings, the palaces, the temples of immortality and glory.

He is risen! He has tasted death, but he has not seen corruption; for he is the Holy One of God, and upon holiness corruption cannot fasten. As the beloved of the Father, he rises from the dead; for the Father loves him because he gives his life for the sheep. And in this resurrection we read the Father's testimony to his Sonship; the Father's seal set to his completed propitiation; the Father's declaration of satisfaction and delight in the work of Calvary.

It was henceforth with a risen Master that the disciples had to do. It was a risen Christ who was their companion on the way to Emmaus; it was a risen Christ who entered the upper chamber with "Peace be unto you" on his lips; it was a risen Christ who appeared to five hundred brethren at once; it was a risen Christ who saluted them by the sea of Galilee and prepared for them their morning meal on the fire of coals; it was a risen Christ with whom they companied during the forty days when he went out and in among them. And it is now with a risen Christ that we have to do in the pathways of our daily pilgrimage. At every turn of the way, resurrection meets us in the person of the Lord Jesus and says to us, "Because I live, you shall live also." For the life that is in him is resurrection life.

It is with this risen life that faith connects us from the moment that we believe in him who died and rose again. Let us note, then, such things as these:

1. *The security of this risen life.* It is not mere life out of nothingness as in the case of the first Adam, but life out of death. And it is this life which Scripture presents to us as higher, fuller, and more secure. The soil out of which the tree of immortality springs is not the common soil of earth; it is the mold of the graveyard, the dust of the tomb. This far securer life, this life that no death can touch, comes to us from the risen life of him who died and rose again. The faith that knits us to him makes us partakers of *his* resurrection life; nay, does it so fully that his resurrection becomes ours: We are risen with him, and with him have put on a divine immortality.

2. *The power of the risen life.* It was as the risen one that he spoke, "All *power* is given unto me." It was as possessor of this power that he went forth from the sepulchre; a power like that by which he overcame death; "the power of an endless life." This corn of wheat had fallen into the ground and died; though sown in weak-

ness, it was raised in power. It was with this power of the risen life that he ascended on high, leading captivity captive. It is this power of the risen life that he now wields upon the throne. It is in this power of the risen life that he comes again in his glory: Redeemer, King, Judge of all. It is this power of the risen life that he puts forth in his Church—that he exercises in the begetting us again to a lively hope, and in sustaining each begotten one in a world of hostility and death, amid fightings without and fears within. It is to the power of this risen life that we betake ourselves in the day of weakness and conflict so that, strong in the Lord and in the power of his might, we are made more than conquerors.

3. *The love of the risen life.* Resurrection was a new and higher stage of being; and with the perfection of the life, there came the perfection of the love. The instrument was now more perfectly tuned and fitted both for containing and giving forth new measures of love. The love of the risen life is the largest and the highest of all. It is of this love that we are made partakers—a love beyond all that is earthly and human, a love that passes knowledge.

4. *The sympathies of the risen life.* Resurrection does not form a gulf or throw up a wall between us and the risen one. It is not the shepherd withdrawing from his flock to some inaccessible height. It is the filling up of every gulf, the throwing down of every wall; it is the shepherd bringing himself into closer and fuller sympathy with his flock. True, they are evil, and he is good; they are earthly, and he is heavenly. But that which resurrection laid aside was not anything of true humanity. It was but the sinless infirmities which weighed down his true humanity and kept its sympathies from coming out into full development and play. The risen life, then, is the life of truest and largest sympathy. In its perfection there is the perfection of sympathy, the development of the full round of fellow feeling existing in the being of the Word made flesh.

5. *The affinities of the risen life.* The resurrection breaks no bonds save those of mortality. It is the strengthening, not the weakening, of the links that fasten the Son of God to us, and us to the Son of God. Resurrection ties are the strongest of all. The risen life of Christ alters none of the affinities between himself and his saints; it has not lessened the number of the points at which we come in contact with him; it has not made him less human, nor stopped certain channels of communication between us and him. His immor-

tality has not unlinked him from those who are still here in flesh. His risen life has not shaken or loosened the relationship he bears to the unrisen. All that he was before, he is still, with something superadded of new love, new power, new perfection, new glory. The difference between his unrisen and his risen life is only that between the sun at dayspring and at noon. Let us rejoice at the remembrance of his risen life as the truest, the fittest, the most blessed for us. The more that we realize our own mortality, the more let us feel the preciousness and the suitableness of his immortality as the risen one; and the more let us realize the identity between us and him, in virtue of which not merely we shall rise, but we have risen with him.

6. *The joys of the risen life.* In the tomb, the man of sorrows left all his sorrows as he left all our sins. There they were buried with him. At his resurrection his full joy began, and in the Psalms this connection between his resurrection and his joy is more than once proclaimed. In Psalm 16 the two things are placed very strikingly together; for after it is said, "You will not allow your Holy One to see corruption," it is added, "You will show me the path of life [resurrection]; in your presence is fulness of joy" (see also Psalms 30:3–5; 116:3–7). For him resurrection was joy, not merely because it ended his connection with death, but because it introduced him into the fulness of joy—a joy peculiar to the risen life and of which only a risen man can be capable. Into the joy of his risen life, we in some measure enter here by faith; but the fulness of that risen joy is yet in reserve for us, awaiting the resurrection of the just when the body as well as the head shall have done with tribulation and with death forever.

7. *The hopes of the risen life.* We are "begotten again to a lively [or living and life-giving] hope by the resurrection of Jesus Christ from the dead" (1 Peter 1:3). With Christ's resurrection and with his risen life our "hope" is connected—a "hope" which contains and imparts "life" here; a "hope" which, like a flower from the bud, opens out into the fulness of the glorious life hereafter. The hope of which we are partakers through the risen life of the second Adam far transcends any hope which the unrisen life of the first Adam could have given. It is the hope of an inheritance, a kingdom, a city, a glory such as belongs only to the risen offspring of the second Adam and such as can be possessed only by the redeemed and the

risen. The resurrection of the Son of God is to us the earnest and the pledge of this blessed hope. Hence our watchword is, "Christ in us, the hope of the glory."

For the Church of God, the words "he is risen" are full of health and gladness. The more that we dwell upon our Surety's resurrection, the more shall we realize the life and immortality which have been brought to light by his Gospel. The oftener that we visit his empty tomb and see for ourselves that he is not here, he is risen, the more shall we be penetrated by that wondrous truth that we are risen with him; and that this fellowship in resurrection is as truly the source of spiritual life, health, and holiness, as it is of joy unspeakable and full of glory.

For each sad sinner, still buried in the grave of sin, the words contain a Gospel—glad tidings of great joy. The empty tomb of Jesus gives forth a voice which reaches to the very ends of the earth. Everlasting life through him who died and rose again; forgiveness and righteousness and reconciliation through the accepted work of the great substitute, finished on the cross, but sealed and attested by resurrection; peace with God through him who left the tomb and went up to the Father's right hand, as at once the maker and the giver of peace—all this we preach without condition or restriction to a world lying in wickedness that each condemned one may hear and live! Through this man is preached unto you the forgiveness of sins! Take the free pardon now; and in taking it, exchange at once, without one moment's delay or uncertainty, life for death, liberty for bondage, sonship for alienation, joy for sorrow, a hope that does not make ashamed, for heaviness here and eternal despair hereafter. He is risen, sinner, he is risen! Go, deal with this risen Christ; go, transact the great business for eternity with him; go, receive life and blessing at his hands. For truly he is the same Savior still as when, by the sea of Galilee, he said to sinners as far off as you can be, "Come unto me, and I will give you rest."

9

THE PARDON AND THE PEACE MADE SURE

"Christ for us," the obedient in the place of the disobedient, is the *first* part of our message. His assumption of the legal claims, which otherwise would have been made good against us, is the security for our deliverance. That deliverance becomes an actual thing to us immediately upon our consenting to allow him to undertake our case.

"Christ in us" is the *second* part of our Gospel. This second is of mighty moment, yet is not to be confounded with the first. That which is done *for* us is not the same as that which is done *in* us. By the former we are constituted righteous; by the latter we are made holy. The one is properly *the Gospel,* in the belief of which we are saved; the other, the carrying out of that Gospel in the soul.

Christ "for us" is our justification. "Christ in us, and we in Christ," is our holiness. The former is the external substitution; the latter, the internal energy or operation, taking its rise from the former, yet not to be confounded with it or substituted for it.

Christ the substitute, giving his life for ours upon the cross, is specially the object of faith. The message concerning this sacrificial work is the Gospel, the belief of which brings pardon to the guilty.

God has given us this Gospel not merely for the purpose of securing to us life hereafter, but of *making us sure* of this life even now. It is a true and sure Gospel so that he who believes it is made sure of being saved. If it could not make us sure, it would make us miserable; for to be told of such a salvation and such a glory, yet kept in doubt as to whether they are to be ours or not, must render us truly wretched. What a poor Gospel it must be which leaves the man who believes it still in doubt as to whether he is a child of God, an unpardoned or a pardoned sinner! Till we have found forgiveness, we cannot be happy; we cannot serve God gladly or lovingly; but must be in sore bondage and gloom.

This is the view of the matter which Scripture sets before us; telling us that salvation is a free, a sure, and a present gift. "He that believes is justified" (Acts 13:39). "He that believes has everlasting life" (John 3:36). The Bible gives no quarter to unbelief or doubting. It does not call it humility. It does not teach us to think better of ourselves for doubting. It does not countenance uncertainty or darkness.

This was the view taken of the subject by our fathers from the Reformation downwards. They held that a man ought to *know* that he is justified; that it was popery to teach uncertainty, or to set aside the full assurance of faith, or to hold that this sureness was not to be had from the beginning of a man's conversion, but only to be gathered up in process of years by summing up his good feelings and good deeds and concluding from his own excellences that he must be one of the elect, a man in favor with God. Our fathers believed that the jailor at Philippi rejoiced as soon as he received the good news which Paul preached to him (Acts 16:34). Our fathers believed that, "being justified by faith, *we have* peace with God" (Romans 5:1), and that the life of a believing man is a life of *known* pardon; a life of peace with God; a life of which the outset was the settlement of the great question between himself and God; a life in which, as being a walk with God, the settlement of that question did not admit of being deferred or kept doubtful. For without *felt* agreement, without *conscious* reconciliation, intercourse was impossible.

All the Reformation creeds and confessions take this for granted; assuming that the doctrine of uncertainty was one of the worst lies of Popery,* the device and stronghold of a money-loving

---

*"What do you think of the doctrine of the Papists, whereby they teach the people to doubt and fear? It is a comfortless doctrine, placing a believer at his departure no higher than an unbeliever" (Heidelberg Catechism). Elsewhere in the same Catechism we have the following quotation: *"What comfort have the Papists here?* Continual doubting, an unquiet mind, and the wreck of conscience. They say:

Three things there are that trouble my mind:
The first, that I the grave must find;
The second troubleth me more yet—

priesthood who wished to keep people in suspense in order to make room for the dealings of priests and payments for pardon. If assurance be the right of every man who believes, then the priest's occupation is at an end; his craft is not only in danger, but gone. It was the want of assurance in his poor victims that enabled him to drive so prosperous a trade and to coin money out of people's doubts. It was by this craft he had his wealth and hence the hatred with which Rome and her priests have always hated the doctrine of assurance. It took the bread out of their mouths. If God pardons so freely, so simply, so surely, so immediately upon believing, alas for the priesthood! Who will pay them for absolution? Who will go to them to make sure that which God has already made sure in a more excellent way than theirs?

Romanists have always maintained that assurance is presumption. It is remarkable that they quote, in defense of their opinion, the same passages which many modern Protestants do, such as, "Work out your salvation with fear and trembling"; the apostle's expression about being "a castaway"; "Let him that thinks he stands"; and the like.

One of them, in reasoning with one of the English Reformers, speaks of "the presumptuous opinion of the certainty of grace and salvation, contrary to that which St. Paul counselleth, Phil. ii. 12." The great Romish controversialists give the following reasons against assurance, which we abridge and translate:

(1) No man certainly ought to disbelieve God's mercy and Christ's merits; but on account of his own imperfections, he ought to be fearful about his own grace, so that no one can certainly know that he has found favor with God.

  That I know not the time of it;
  The third above all troubleth me—
  That whither I must I cannot see.
What doth a believer set against this?
  Three things there are that cheer my mind:
  First, that in Christ I pardon find;
  The second cheers me much more yet—
  That Christ my Lord for me is fit;
  The third above all cheereth me—
  That I my place in Heaven do see."

(2) It is not expedient that men should have certainty about their own grace; for certainty produces pride, while ignorance of this secret preserves and increases humility.

(3) Assurance is the privilege of only a few favored ones to whom God has revealed the singular benefit of the pardon of their sins.

(4) The most perfect men, when dying, have been humbled because of this uncertainty; and if some of the honest men have been uncertain, is it credible that all believers ought to have assurance of their justification?

(5) The best men may fall from faith; therefore, there can be no assurance.

(6) The following passages confute the error of assurance: 1 Corinthians 10:12; 2 Corinthians 6:1; Romans 11:20; Philippians 2:12.

Such are the popish arguments against assurance. The conclusion to which the Council of Trent came was: "If any man shall say that justifying faith is confidence in the mercy of God, who remitteth sins for Christ's sake, or that it is by such confidence alone that we are justified, let him be accursed."

Old John Foxe, who three hundred years ago wrote the history of the martyrs, remarks concerning the Pope's Church, that it "left the poor consciences of men in perpetual doubt" (vol. 1, p. 78).

This is a true saying. But it is true of many who earnestly protest against the Church of Rome. They not only teach doctrines which necessarily lead to doubting and out of which no poor sinner could extract anything but uncertainty; but they inculcate doubting as a humble and excellent thing; a good preparation, even an indispensable qualification, for faith. The duty of doubting is in their theology much more obligatory than that of believing. The propriety and necessity of being uncertain they strongly insist upon; the blessedness of certainty they undervalue; the sin of uncertainty they repudiate; the duty of being sure they deny.

This same John Foxe, after showing that a man is saved not by working but by believing, gives us the following specimen of "the horrible blindness and blasphemy" of the Church of Rome:

> That faith wherewith a man firmly believeth and certainly assureth himself, that for Christ's sake his sins be forgiven him,

and that he shall possess eternal life, is not faith, but rashness; not the persuasion of the Holy Ghost, but the presumption of human audacity.

The above extract is from a popish book of the time and is a fair specimen of the Romish hatred of the doctrine of assurance. Its language is almost the same as that employed by many Protestants of our day.

The Romanists held that a man is to believe in the mercy of God and the merits of Christ, but that this belief brought with it no assurance of justification; though possibly—if the man lived a very holy life—God might before he died reveal his grace to him and give him assurance. This is precisely what many Protestants hold.

In opposition to this our forefathers not only maintained that a man is justified by faith, but that he ought to *know that he is justified,* and that this knowledge of justification is the great root of a holy life. The Romanists did not quarrel with the word *assurance;* they did not hold it to be impossible: They held that men *might* get it, even that some very holy men had got it. But they affirmed that the only means of reaching the grace of assurance was by a holy life; that with the slow development of a holy life, assurance might develop itself; and that in the course of years, a man by numbering his good deeds, and ascertaining the amount of his holiness, might *perhaps* come to the conclusion that he was a child of God; but perhaps not. They were very strenuous in contending for this life of *religious suspense*—sad and dismal as it must be—because *conscious justification,* such as Luther contended for, shut out priesthood and penance; giving a man the joy of true liberty and divine fellowship at once without the intervention of another party or the delay of an hour.

This *conscious* justification started the man upon a happy life because relieved from the burden of doubt and the gloom of uncertainty, it made his religion bright and tranquil; because springing so sweetly from the certainty of his reconciliation to God, it delivered him from the cruel suspense and undefined fears which the want of assurance carries always with it. It rescued him from all temptations to self-righteousness, because, not arising from any good thing in himself, it preserved him from pride and presumption; because it kept him from trying to magnify his own goodness in order to extract assurance out of it, it drew him away from self to Christ—from what *he* was doing to what *Christ* had done; thus making Christ, not self, the basis and the center of his new being. It made him more and more dissatisfied with self, and all that self contained, but more and more satisfied with Jesus and his fulness. It taught him to rest his confidence toward God, not on his satisfaction with self, not on the development of his own holiness, not on the amount of his graces and prayers and doings, but simply on the completed work of him in whom God is well-pleased.

The Romanists acquiesced in the general formula of the Protestants—that salvation was all of Christ, and that we are to believe on him in order to get it. But they resisted the idea that a man, on believing, knows that he is saved. They might even have admitted the term "justification by faith," provided it was conceded that this justification was to be known only to God, hidden from the sinner who believes. They did not much heed the mere form of words, and some of them went apparently a long way to the Protestant doctrine. But that which was essential to their system was that in whatever way justification took place, it should be kept secret from the sinner himself so that he should remain without assurance for years, perhaps all his life. *Unconscious justification by faith* suited their system of darkness quite as well as *justification by works*. For it was not merely the kind of justification that they hated, but *the sinner's knowing* it and having peace with God simply in believing without waiting for years of doing. No doubt they objected to free justification in the Protestant sense; but the force of their objection lies not so much against its being *free*, as against the sinner being *sure* of it. For they saw well enough that if they could only introduce *uncertainty* at any part of the process, their end was gained. For to remove such uncertainty the Church must be called in, and this was all they wanted.

The doctrine, then, that makes uncertainty necessary and that affirms that this uncertainty can only be removed by the development of a holy life, is the old popish one, though uttered by Protestants. Luther condemned it; Bellarmine maintained it. And many of the modern objections to assurance, on the part of some Protestants, are a mere reproduction of old Romish arguments, urged again and again, against justification by faith.

There is hardly one objection made to a man's being sure of his justification which would not apply, and which has not been applied, against his being justified by faith at all. If the common arguments against assurance turn out valid, they cannot stop short of establishing *justification by works*. Salvation by believing, and assurance only by means of working, are not very compatible.

The interval which is thus created between God's act of justifying us and his letting us know that he has justified us is a singular one of which Scripture certainly takes no cognizance. This interval of suspense (be it longer or shorter) which Romanists have created for the purpose of giving full scope to priestly interposition and which some Protestants keep up in order to save us from pride and presumption, is not acknowledged in the Bible any more than purgatory. An intermediate state *in the life to come* during which the soul is neither pardoned nor unpardoned, neither in Heaven nor Hell, is thought needful by Romanists for purging out sin and developing holiness; but this interval of gloom is one of man's creation. An intermediate state *in this life* during which a sinner, though believing in Jesus, is not to know whether he is justified or not, is reckoned equally needful by some Protestants as a necessary means of producing holiness and, through holiness, leading perhaps, ere life close, to assurance; but then of this sorrowful interval, this present purgatory, which would make a Christian's life so dreary and fearful, the Scripture says nothing. It is a human delusion borrowed from popery and based upon the dislike of the human heart to have immediate peace, immediate adoption, and immediate fellowship.

The self-righteous heart of man craves an interval of the above kind as a space for the exercise of his religiousness while free from the responsibility for a holy and unworldly life which *conscious* justification imposes on the conscience.

But it will be greatly worth our while to see what Romanists have said upon this subject, for their errors help us much in understanding the truth. It will be seen that it was against present peace with God that Rome contended; and that it was in defense of this present peace, this immediate certainty, that the Reformers did battle so strenuously as a matter of life and death. The great Popish Assembly, the "Council of Trent," in 1547, took up these points concerning faith and grace. Nor was that body content with *condemning* assurance; they proclaimed it an accursed thing and pronounced an anathema against everyone who affirmed that justifying faith is "confidence in the mercy of God." They denounced the man as a heretic who should hold "the confidence and certainty of the remission of his sins."

Yet they had a theory of a justification by faith. We give it in their own words, as it corresponds strikingly with the process which is prescribed by some Protestants as the means of arriving, after long years, at the knowledge of our justification:

> The beginning of justification proceedeth from preventing grace. The manner of the preparation is, first to believe the divine revelations and promises, and knowing oneself to be a sinner, to turn from the fear of God's justice to his mercy, to hope for pardon from him, and therefore to begin to love him and hate sin, to begin a new life, and keep the commandments of God. Justification follows this preparation.

This theory of a gradual justification, or a gradual approach to justification, is that held by many Protestants and made use of by them for resisting the truth of immediate forgiveness of sin and peace with God.

Then comes another sentence of the Council, which expresses truly the modern theory of non-assurance and the common excuse for doubting when men say, "We are not doubting Christ; we are only doubting ourselves." The Romish divines assert:

> No one ought to doubt the mercy of God, the merits of Christ, and the efficacy of the sacraments; but in regard to his own indisposition he may doubt, because *he cannot know by certainty, of infallible faith*, that he has obtained grace.

Here sinners are taught to believe in God's mercy and in Christ's merits, yet still to go on doubting as to the results of that belief; namely, sure peace with God. Truly self-righteousness, whether resting on works or on feelings, whether in Popery or Protestantism, is the same thing, the root of the same errors, and the source of the same determination not to allow immediate certainty to the sinner from the belief of the good news.

This Popish Council took special care that the doctrine of assurance should be served with their most pointed curses. All the "errors of Martin" were by them traced back to this two-fold root, that a man is justified. They thus accuse the German Reformer of *inventing* his doctrine of immediate and conscious justification for the purpose of destroying the sinner's works of repentance, which by their necessary imperfection make room for indulgences. They call this free justification, a thing unheard of before—a thing which not only makes good works unnecessary, but sets a man free from any obligation to obey the law of God.

It would appear that the learned doctors of the Council were bewildered with the Lutheran doctrine. The schoolmen had never discussed it, nor even stated it. It had no place either among the beliefs or misbeliefs of the past. It had not been maintained as a truth, nor impugned as a heresy, so far as they knew. It was an absolute novelty. They did not comprehend it and of course misrepresented it. As to original sin, *that* had been so often discussed by the schoolmen that all Romish divines and priests were familiar with it in one aspect or another. On it, therefore, the Council were at home and could frame their curses easily and with some point. But the Lutheran doctrine of justification brought them to a stand. Thus the old translator of Paul Sarpi's *History* puts it:

> The opinion of Luther concerning justifying faith, that it is a confidence and certain persuasion of the promise of God, with the consequences that follow, of the distinction between the law and the gospel, etc., had never been thought of by any school writers, and therefore never confuted or discussed, so that the divines had work enough to understand the meaning of the Lutheran propositions.

Luther's doctrine of the will's bondage they were indignant at as making man a stone or a machine. His doctrine of righteousness by faith horrified them as the inlet of all laxity and wickedness. Protestant doctrines were to them absurdities no less than heresies.

Nor was it merely the church, the Fathers, and tradition that they stood upon. The schools and the schoolmen! This was their watchword; for hitherto these scholastic doctors had been, at least for centuries, the bodyguard of the church. Under their learning and subtleties and casuistries, priests and bishops had always taken refuge. Indeed, without them the church was helpless so far as logic was concerned. When she had to argue, she must call in these metaphysical divines; though generally by force and terror she contrived to supersede all necessity for reasoning.

Three men in the Council showed some independence: a Dominican friar, by name Ambrosius Catarinus; a Spanish Franciscan, by name Andreas de Vega; and a Carmelite, by name Antonius Marinarus. The "Heremites" of the order to which Luther originally belonged were especially blind and bitter, their leader Seripandus outdoing all in zeal against Luther and his heresy.

Compelled in the investigation of the subject to pass beyond Luther to Luther's master, they were sorely puzzled. To overlook him was impossible, for the Protestants appealed to him; to condemn him would not have been wise.

They were obliged to admit the bitter truth that Paul had said that a man is justified by faith. They had maintained the strict literality of "This is my body"; must they admit the equal literality of "justified by faith"? Or may this latter expression not be qualified and overlaid by scholastic ingenuity, or set aside by an authoritative denial in the name of the church? At the Council of Trent both these methods were tried.

It was not Luther only who laid such stress upon the doctrine of free justification. His adversaries were wise enough to do the same. They saw in it the root or foundation stone of the whole Reformation. If it falls, popery stands erect and may do what she pleases with the consciences of men. If it stands, popery is overthrown; her hold on men's consciences is gone; her priestly power is at an end, and men have directly to do with the Lord Jesus Christ in Heaven and not with any pretended vicar upon Earth, or any of his priests or seven sacraments. "All the errors of Martin are resolved into that point," said the bishops of the Council; and they added, "He that will establish the Catholic doctrine must overthrow the heresy of righteousness by faith only."

But did not Paul say the same things as Luther has said? Did he not say, *"To him that works not, but believes* on him that justifies the ungodly, his faith is counted for righteousness"? (Romans 4:5).

Yes, but we may use some liberties with Paul's words which we cannot do with Luther's. It would not do to refute Paul, but it is quite safe to demonstrate that Luther is wrong and is at variance with the church.

Let us then assail Luther, and leave Paul alone. Now Luther has said such things as the following:

1. Faith without works is sufficient for salvation and alone justifies.

2. Justifying faith is a sure trust by which one believes that his sins are remitted for Christ's sake, and they that are justified are to believe certainly that their sins are remitted.

3. By faith only we are able to appear before God, who neither regards nor has need of our works; faith only purifying us.

4. No previous disposition is necessary to justification; neither does faith justify because it disposes us, but because it is a means or instrument by which the promise and grace of God are laid hold on and received.

5. All the works of men, even the most sanctified, are sin.

6. Though the just ought to believe that his works are sins, yet he ought to be assured that they are not imputed.

7. Our righteousness is nothing but the imputation of the righteousness of Christ, and the just have need of a continual justification and imputation of the righteousness of Christ.

8. All the justified are received into equal grace and glory, and all Christians are equally great with the mother of God and as much saints as she.

These were some of Luther's propositions, which required to be confuted. That they looked wonderfully like the doctrines of the Apostle Paul only made the confutation more necessary. That "faith justifies," the bishops said, we must admit because the apostle has said so; but as to what faith is, and how it justifies, is hard to say. Faith has many meanings (some said nine, others fifteen; some modern Protestants have said the same); and then, even admitting that faith justifies, it cannot do so without good dispositions, without penance, without religious performances, without sacraments. By introducing all these ingredients into faith, they easily turned it into a work; or by placing them on the same level with faith, they nullified (without positively denying) justification by faith.

Ingenious men! Thus to overthrow the truth, while professing to admit and explain it! In this ingenious perversity they have had many successors, and that in churches which rejected Rome and its Council.

"Christ crucified" is the burden of the message which God has sent to man. "Christ died for our sins, according to the Scriptures." The reception of this Gospel is eternal life; the non-reception or rejection of it is everlasting death. "This is the record, that God has given to us eternal life, and this life is in His Son." The belief of the Gospel saves; the belief of the promise annexed to that Gospel makes us sure of this salvation personally. It is not *the belief of our belief* that assures us of pardon and gives us a good conscience toward God; *but our belief of what God has promised to everyone who believes his Gospel*—that is eternal life. "Believe in the Lord Jesus Christ, and *you shall be saved.*"

What is God to me? That is the first question that rises up to an inquiring soul. And the second is like unto it: What am I to God? On these two questions hangs all religion, as well as all joy and life to the immortal spirit.

If God is for me, and I am for God, all is well. If God is not for me, and if I am not for God, all is ill (Romans 8:31). If he takes my side, and if I take his, there is nothing to fear—either in this world or in that which is to come. If he is not on my side, and if I am not on his, then what can I do but fear? Terror in such a case must be as natural and inevitable as in a burning house or a sinking vessel.

Or, *if I do not know* whether God is for me or not, I can have no rest. In a matter such as this, my soul seeks certainty; not uncertainty. I must *know* that God is for me, else I must remain in the sadness of unrest and terror. Insofar as my actual safety is concerned, everything depends on God being for me; and insofar as my present peace is concerned, everything depends on my *knowing* that God is for me. Nothing can calm the tempest of my soul save the knowledge that I am his, and that he is mine.

Our relationship to God is then to us the first question; till this is settled, nothing else can be settled. It is the question of questions to us, in comparison with which all other personal questions are as moonshine. When the health of a beloved child is in danger, I seem for the time to lose sight of everything around me while wholly absorbed in the thought, Will he live, or will he die? I move about the house as one who sees nothing, hears nothing. I go to and I come from the sickroom incessantly; watching every symptom for the better or the worse. I eagerly inquire at the physician, Is there hope, or is there none? I am paralyzed in everything and indifferent to the things which in other circumstances might interest me. What matters it to me whether it rains or shines, whether my garden flowers are fading or flourishing, whether I am losing or making money, so long as I am uncertain whether that beloved child is to live or die?

And if uncertainty as to my child's health be so important to me, and so engrossing as to make me forget everything else; oh, what must be the engrossment attending the unsettled question of the life or death of my own immortal soul! I must *know* that my child is out of danger before I can rest, and I must *know* that my soul is out of danger before I can be quieted in spirit. *Suspense* in such case is terrible; and, were our eyes fully open to the eternal peril, absolutely *unendurable*. *Not to know* whether we are out of danger must be as fatal to peace of soul as the certainty of danger itself. Suspense as to temporal calamities has often in a night withered the fresh cheek of youth and turned the golden hair to grey. And shall time's uncertainties work such havoc with their transient terrors, and shall eternal uncertainties pass over us as the idle wind?

In the great things of eternity nothing but *certainty* will do. Nothing but *certainty* can soothe our fears or set us free to attend to the various questions of lesser moment which every hour brings up. The man who can continue to go about these lesser things while *uncertainty* still hangs over his everlasting prospects and the great question between his soul and God is still unsettled must be either sadly hardened or altogether wretched.

He who remains in this uncertainty remains a burdened and weary man. He who is contented with this uncertainty is contented with misery and danger. He who clings to this uncertainty as a *right thing* can have no pretensions to the name of son, or child, or saint of God. For in that uncertainty, is there any feature of resemblance to the son or the saint; anything of the spirit of adoption, whereby we cry, Abba, Father; any likeness to the filial spirit of the beloved Son of God?

He who resolves to remain in this uncertainty is a destroyer of his own soul, and he who tries to persuade others to remain in this uncertainty is a murderer of souls. He who does his best to make himself comfortable without the knowledge of his reconciliation and relationship to God is a manifest unbeliever, and he who tries to induce others to be comfortable without this knowledge is something worse—if worse can be. That there are many among professing

Christians who have not this knowledge is a painful fact; that there are some who, instead of lamenting this, make their boast of it is a fact more painful still; that there are even some who proclaim their own uncertainty in order to countenance others in it is a fact the most painful of all.

Thus the questions about assurance resolve themselves into that of the knowledge of our relationship to God. To an Arminian, who denies election and the perseverance of the saints, the knowledge of our present reconciliation to God might bring with it no assurance of final salvation. According to him, we may be in reconciliation today and out of it tomorrow. To a Calvinist there can be no such separation. He who is once reconciled is reconciled forever; the knowledge of filial relationship just now is the assurance of eternal salvation. Indeed, apart from God's electing love, there can be no such thing as assurance. It becomes an impossibility.

By nature we have no peace: "There is no peace to the wicked." Man craves peace, longs for it. God has made it for us and presents it to us.

Many are the causes of dispeace; sin is the root of all. Where unpardoned sin is, there cannot be peace. Many are the subordinate causes. An empty soul, disappointment, wounded affection, worldly losses, bereavement, vexations, cares, weariness of spirit, broken hopes, deceitful friendships, our own blunders and failures, the misconduct or unkindnesses of others. These produce dispeace; these are the winds that ruffle the surface of life's sea.

Many are the efforts and appliances to obtain peace. Man's whole life is filled up with these. His daily cry is, "Give me peace!" He tries to get it in such ways as the following:

1. *By forgetting God.* It is the remembrance of God that troubles a sinner. He could get over many of his disquietudes if he could keep God at a distance. He tries to thrust him out of his thoughts, his heart, his mind, his conscience. Though he could succeed, what would it avail? He would only bring himself more surely into the number of those who shall be "turned into Hell," for they are they who "forget God." What will forgetting God do for a soul? What will it avail to thrust him out of our thoughts?

2. *By following the world.* The heart must be filled by someone or in some way. Man betakes himself to the world as that which is most congenial and most likely to satisfy his cravings. Pleasure,

gaiety, business, folly, change, gold, friends—these man tries; but in vain. Peace comes not.

3. *By working hard and denying self.* The dispeace of a troubled conscience comes from the thought of evil deeds done or good deeds left undone. This dispeace he tries to remove by trying to shake off the evil that is in him and to introduce the good that is not in him. But the hard labor is fruitless. It does not pacify the conscience or assure him of pardon, without which there can be no peace.

4. *By being very religious.* He does not know that true religion is the fruit or result of peace found, not the way to it or the price paid for it. He may be on his knees from morn till night, and may make long fastings and vigils, or prosecute his devotional performances till body and soul are worn out; but all will not do. Peace is as far off as ever.

He wants peace; but he takes his own way of getting it, not God's. He thinks there is a resting place; but he overlooks the free love that said, "Come unto me, and I will give you rest."*

The peace of the cross, what is it? What does it do for us?

What is it? It is peace of conscience, peace with God, peace with the law of God, peace with the holiness of God. It is reconciliation, friendship, fellowship; and all this in a way which prevents the dread or possibility of future variance or distance or condemnation. For it is not simply *peace,* but the peace of the cross; peace extracted from the cross; peace founded on and derived from what the cross reveals and what the cross has done. It is peace whose basis

---

*"I believe these words on the divine testimony. My conscience bears witness to their truth. It is a good conscience; it agrees with God; and looks upon him as reconciled perfectly. It fears to dishonor him by calling in question the infinite value of Christ's righteousness and atonement, or doubting of their being mine, while they are freely offered to me, while I find my want of them, and have my dependence upon them. Thus the peace of God rules, takes the lead in the conscience, rules always, the offer being always the same, the righteousness and atonement of Jesus always the same, my want of them always the same, and mine interest in them always the same; which I daily learn to maintain by all means, against all corruptions, enemies, and temptations from every quarter."

is forgiveness, "no condemnation." It is peace which comes from our knowledge of the peacemaking work of Calvary. It is *true* peace, *sure* peace, *present* peace, *righteous* peace, *divine* peace, *heavenly* peace, the peace of God, the peace of Christ, complete peace, pervading the whole being.

What does it do for us?

1. *It calms our storms.* In us tempests rage perpetually. The storms of the unforgiven spirit are the most fearful of all: whirlwind, earthquake, rushing blast, lightning, raging waves—these are the emblems of a human heart. But peace comes, and all is still. The great Peacemaker comes, and there is a great calm. The holy pardon which he bestows is the messenger of rest.

2. *It removes our burdens.* A sinner's heaviest burdens must ever be dread of God, lack of conscious reconciliation with him, uncertainty as to the eternal future. Peace with God is the end of all these. A sight of the cross relieves us of our burdens, and connection with the sin bearer assures us that these shall never be laid on us again.

3. *It breaks our bonds.* Sharp and heavy are the chains of sin, not merely because sin is a disease preying upon our spiritual nature, but because it is guilt which must be answered for before a righteous Judge. Unpardoned guilt is both prison and fetters. Forgiveness brings with it peace, and with peace every chain is broken. Our prison doors are opened; we walk forth into liberty.

4. *It strengthens us for warfare.* Without peace we cannot fight. Our hands hang down, and our weapons fall from them. Our courage is gone. So long as God is our enemy, or so long as we know not whether God is our friend, we are disabled men. We are without heart and without hope. But when reconciliation comes and God becomes our assured friend, then we are strong, well nerved for battle, fearless in the conflict, full of hope and heart. "If God be for us, who can be against us?"

5. *It cheers us in trial.* The peace of God within is our chiefest consolation when sorrows crowd in upon us. Lighted up with this true lamp, we are not greatly moved because of the darkness without. Peace with God is our anchor in the storm, our strong tower in adverse times, the soother of our hearts, and the dryer-up of our tears. We learn to call affliction light, and to find that it works for us an exceeding and eternal weight of glory.

Is my soul at rest? If so, whence has the rest come? If not, why is it not at rest? Is *unrest* a necessity after Christ has said, "I will give you rest"?

Am I satisfied with the Gospel? Is my heart content with Christ himself and my conscience with what he has done? If *not* content, why? What bothers me about him and his work? Would I have something added to that work, or something taken from it? Is it not, at this moment, exactly the thing for me; exactly the thing which contains all the peace and rest I need? And am I not, at this moment, exactly the person whom it suits; to whom, without any change or delay, it offers all its fulness?

The propitiation and the righteousness finished on the cross, and there exhibited as well as presented to me freely, are such as entirely meet my case: offering me all that which is fitted to remove dispeace and unrest from heart and conscience; revealing as they do the free love of God to the sinner and providing for the removal of every hindrance in the way of that love flowing down; proclaiming aloud the rent veil, the open way, the gracious welcome, the plenteous provision, and the everlasting life.

Peace does not save us, yet it is the portion of a saved soul.

Assurance does not save us; they have erred who have spoken of assurance as indispensable to salvation. For we are not saved by believing in our own salvation, nor by believing anything whatsoever about ourselves. We are saved by what we believe about the Son of God and his righteousness. The Gospel believed saves, not the believing in our own faith.

Nevertheless, let us know that assurance was meant to be the portion of every believing sinner. It was intended not merely that he should be saved, but that he should *know* that he is saved, and so delivered from all fear and bondage and heaviness of heart.

10

THE HOLY LIFE OF THE JUSTIFIED

"To him that *works not,* but *believes,*" says the apostle speaking of the way in which we are reckoned just before God.

Does he by this speech make light of good works? Does he encourage an unholy walk? Does he use a rash word which had better been left unspoken?

No, truly. He is laying the foundation of good works. He is removing the great obstacle to a holy life, namely, the bondage of an unforgiven state. He is speaking, by the power of the Holy Ghost, the words of truth and soberness. The difference between working and believing is that which God would have us learn, lest we confound these two things and so destroy them both. The order and relation of these two things are here very explicitly laid down so as to anticipate the error of many who mix up working and believing together or who make believing the result of working, instead of working the result of believing.

We carefully distinguish, yet we as carefully connect the two. We do not put asunder what God has joined together; yet we would not reverse the divine order, nor disturb the divine relation, nor place that last which God has set first.

It was not to depreciate or discourage good works that the apostle spoke of "not working, but believing," or of a man being "justified by faith, *without the deeds of the law*" (Romans 3:28), or of God "imputing righteousness *without works*" (4:6). It was to distinguish things that differ; it was to show the true use of faith in connecting us for justification with what another has done; it was to prevent us from *doing* anything in order to be justified. In this view, then, faith is truly a ceasing from work, and not a working; it is not the doing of anything in order to be justified, but the simple reception of the justifying work of him who "finished transgression and made an end of sin." For *the one justifying work* was completed eighteen hundred years ago, and any attempt on our part to repeat or imitate this is vain. The one cross suffices.

Nor was it to undervalue good works that our Lord gave what many may deem such a singular answer to the question of the Jews, "What shall we do, that we may work the works of God?" "This is the work of God, *that you believe* on him whom he hath sent" (John 6:29). They wanted to work their way into the favor of God. The Lord tells them that they may have that favor without waiting or working by accepting at once his testimony to his only begotten Son. Till then, they were not in a condition for working. They were as trees without a root and as stars whose motions, however regular, would be useless if they themselves were unlighted.

To say to a groping, troubled spirit, You must first believe before you can work, is no more to encourage ungodliness or laxity of walk than to say to an imprisoned soldier, You must first get out of your dungeon before you can fight; or to a swimmer, You must throw off that millstone before you can attempt to swim; or to a racer, You must get quit of these fetters before you can run the race.

Yet these expressions of the apostle have often been shrunk from; dreaded as dangerous; quoted with a guarding clause or cited as seldom as possible under the secret feeling that, unless greatly diluted or properly qualified, they had better not be cited at all. But why are these bold utterances there, if they are perilous, if they are not meant to be as fearlessly proclaimed now as they were fearlessly written eighteen centuries ago? What did the Holy Spirit mean by the promulgation of such "unguarded" statements, as some seem disposed to reckon them? It was not for nothing that they were so boldly spoken. Timid words would not have served the purpose. The glorious Gospel needed statements such as these to disentangle the great question of acceptance and to relieve troubled consciences and purge them from dead works, yet at the same time to give to works their proper place.

Perhaps some of Luther's statements are too unqualified. Yet their very strength shows how much he felt the necessity of so speaking of works as absolutely and preemptorily to exclude them from the office of justifying the sinner. He saw and testified how the Papacy, by mixing the two things together, had troubled and terrified men's consciences and had truly become a "slaughterhouse of souls."

In another's righteousness we stand, and by another's righteousness we are justified. All accusations against us, founded upon our unrighteousness, we answer by pointing to the perfection of the righteousness which covers us from head to foot, in virtue of which we are unassailable by law as well as shielded from wrath.

Protected by this perfection, we have no fear of wrath, either now or hereafter. It is a buckler to us, and we cry, "Behold, O God, our shield; look upon the face of your Anointed"; as if to say, Look not on me, but on my substitute; deal not with me for sin, but with my sin bearer; challenge not me for my guilt, but challenge *him; he* will answer for me. Thus we are safe beneath the shield of his righteousness. No arrow, either from the enemy or from conscience, can reach us there.

Covered by this perfection, we are at peace. The enemy cannot invade us; or if he try to do so, we can triumphantly repel him. It is a refuge from the storm, a covert from the tempest, a river of water in a dry place, the shadow of a great rock in a weary land. The work of righteousness is peace, and in the Lord we have righteousness and strength.

Beautified with this perfection, which is the perfection of God, we find favor in his sight. His eye rests on the comeliness which he has put upon us; and as he did at viewing the first creation, so now, in looking at us clothed with this divine excellency, he pronounces it "very good." He sees "no iniquity in Jacob, and no transgression in Israel." "The iniquity of Jacob may be sought for, and there shall be none; and the sins of Judah, and they shall not be found" (Jeremiah 50:20). This righteousness suffices to cover, to comfort, and to beautify.*

---

*Every time we say "for your name's sake," or "for Christ's sake," we are making use of another's claim, another's merit, and conceding or accepting the whole doctrine of imputed righteousness. Every man is daily getting, in some way or other, what he personally has no title to. When a son gets an inheritance from his father, he gets what does not belong to him and what could easily and legally be diverted from him. When one who is not a son gets an estate by *will,* he gets what he has no claim to simply by a legal deed. Human jurisprudence recognizes these transferences as competent and proper, not fictitious or absurd. Man daily acts on these principles of getting what he has no right to simply because a fellow man wills it, and law acknowledges that will. Why then should he speak of *fictitious* transferences in spiritual blessings proceeding on pre-

But there is more than this. We are justified *that we may be holy.* The possession of this legal righteousness is the beginning of a holy life. We do not live a holy life in order to be justified, but we are justified that we may live a holy life. That which *man* calls holiness may be found in almost any circumstances—of dread, or darkness, or bondage, or self-righteous toil and suffering; but that which God calls holiness can only be developed under conditions of liberty and light, and pardon and peace with God. Forgiveness is the mainspring of holiness. Love, as a motive, is far stronger than law and far more influential than fear of wrath or peril of Hell. Terror may make a man crouch like a slave and obey a hard master lest a worse thing come upon him, but only a sense of forgiving love can bring either heart or conscience into that state in which obedience is either pleasant to the soul or acceptable to God.

False ideas of holiness are common, not only among those who profess false religions, but among those who profess the true. For holiness is a thing of which man by nature has no more idea than a blind man has of the beauty of a flower or the light of the sun. All false religions have had their "holy men" whose holiness often consisted merely in the amount of pain they could inflict upon their bodies, or of food which they could abstain from, or of hard labor which they could undergo. But with God, a saint or holy man is a very different being. It is in filial, full-hearted love to God that much of true holiness consists. And this cannot even *begin* to be until the sinner has found forgiveness and tasted liberty and has confidence towards God. The spirit of holiness is incompatible with the spirit of bondage. There must be the spirit of liberty, the spirit of adoption, whereby we cry, Abba, Father. When the fountain of holiness begins to well up in the human heart and to fill the whole being with its transforming, purifying power, "We have known and believed the love that God has to us" (1 John 4:16) is the first note of the holy song which, commenced on Earth, is to be perpetuated through eternity.

---

cisely the same principle? Why should he deny the law or process of the divine jurisprudence by which forgiveness of sin is conferred on him according to the will of another and secured to him by the claims of another? If earthly law deals thus with him in earthly things, why should not heavenly law deal thus with him in heavenly things?

We are bought with a price that we may be new creatures in Jesus Christ. We are forgiven, that we may be like him who forgives us. We are set at liberty and brought out of prison that we may be holy. The free, boundless love of God pouring itself into us, expands and elevates our whole being; and we serve him, not in order to win his favor, but because we have already won it in simply believing his record concerning his Son. If the root is holy, so are the branches. We have become connected with the holy root and by the necessity of this connection are made holy too.

Forgiveness relaxes no law, nor interferes with the highest justice. Human pardons may often do so; God's pardons never.

Forgiveness doubles all our bonds to a holy life; only they are no longer bonds of iron, but of gold. It takes off the heavy yoke in order to give us the light and easy.

Love is stronger than law. Whatever connects our obedience with love must be far more influential than what connects us with law.

The love of God to us, and our love to God, work together for producing holiness in us. Terror accomplishes no real obedience. Suspense brings forth no fruit unto holiness. Only the certainty of love, forgiving love, can do this. It is this certainty that melts the heart, dissolves our chains, disburdens our shoulders so that we stand erect, and makes us to run in the way of the divine commandments.

Condemnation is that which binds sin and us together. Forgiveness looses this fearful tie and separates us from sin. The power of condemnation which the law possesses is that which makes it so strong and terrible. Cancel this power, and the liberated spirit rises into the region of love. In that region it finds both will and strength for the keeping of the law—a law which is at once old and new, old as to substance ("You shall love the Lord with all your heart") and new as to mode and motive ("The law of the Spirit of life in Christ Jesus has made me free from the law of sin and death" Romans 8:2); that is, the law of the life-giving Spirit which we have in Christ Jesus has served the condemning connection of that law which leads only to sin and death. "For what the law could not do, in that it was weak through the flesh [*i.e.* unable to carry out its commandments in our old nature], God sending his own Son in the likeness of sinful flesh, and for sin, condemned sin in the flesh; that *the righteousness of the law* might be fulfilled in us, who walk not after the flesh, but after the Spirit" (Romans 8:3, 4).

The removal of condemnation is the dissolution of legal bondage and of that awful pressure upon the conscience which at once enslaved and irritated; disenabling as well as disinclining us from all obedience; making holiness both distasteful and dreadful, to be submitted to only through fear of future woe.

Sin, when unforgiven, oppresses the conscience and tyrannizes over the sinner. Sin forgiven in an unrighteous way would be but a slight and uncertain as well as imperfect relief. Sin righteously and judicially forgiven loses its dominion. The conscience rises up from its long oppression and expands into joyous liberty. Our whole being becomes bright and buoyant under the benign influence of this forgiving love of God. "The winter is past, the rain is over and gone, the flowers appear on the earth, the time of the singing of birds is come" (Song of Solomon 2:11, 12).

Condemnation is the dark cloud that obscures our heavens. Forgiveness is the sunshine dissolving the cloud and by its brilliance making all good things to grow and ripen in us.

Condemnation makes sin strike its roots deeper and deeper. No amount of terror can extirpate evil. No fear of wrath can make us holy. No gloomy uncertainty as to God's favor can subdue one lust or correct our crookedness of will. But the free pardon of the cross uproots sin and withers all its branches. The "no condemnation to them that are in Christ Jesus" is the only effectual remedy for the deadly disease of an alienated heart and stubborn will.

The lack of forgiveness, or uncertainty as to it, are barriers in the way of the removal of the heart's deep enmity to a righteous God. For enmity will only give way to love; and no suspense, however terrible, will overcome the stout-hearted rebelliousness of man. Threats do not conquer hearts, nor does austerity win either confidence or affection. They who would rely on law to awaken trust know nothing either of law or love, nor do they understand how the suspicions of the human heart are to be removed and its confidence won. The knowledge of God simply as Judge or Lawgiver will be of no power to attract, of no avail to remove distrust and dread.

But the message, "God is love," is like the sun bursting through the clouds of a long tempest. The good news, "Through this man is preached unto you the forgiveness of sins," is like the opening of the prisoner's dungeon gate. Bondage departs, and liberty comes. Suspicion is gone, and the heart is won. "Perfect love has cast out fear." We hasten to the embrace of him who loved us; we hate that which has estranged us; we put away all that caused the distance between us and him; we long to be like one so perfect and to partake of his holiness. To be "partakers of the divine nature" (2 Peter 1:4), once so distasteful, is henceforth most grateful and pleasant; nothing seems now so desirable as to escape the corruptions that are in the world through lust.

We undergo many false changes which look like holiness, but which are not really so. The poison tree drops its leaves, yet remains the same. The sea of Sodom glistens in the sunshine with surpassing splendor, yet remains salt and bitter as before. Time changes us, yet does not make us holy. The decays of age change us, but do not break the power of evil. One lust expels another; frailty succeeds to frailty; error drives out error. One vanity pales, another comes freshly in its place; one evil habit is exchanged for a second, but our old man remains the same. The cross has not touched us with its regenerating power; the Holy Spirit has not purified the inner sources of our being and life.*

Fashion changes us; the example of friends changes us; society changes us; excitement changes us; business changes us; affection changes us; sorrow changes us; dread of coming evil changes us; yet the heart is just what it was. Of the numerous changes in our character or deportment, how many are deceitful, how few are real and deep!

Only that which can go down into the very depths of our spiritual being can produce any change that is worthy of the name.

---

*"All divine life, and all the precious fruits of it, pardon, peace, and holiness, spring from the cross. . . . Holiness as well as pardon is to be had from the blood of the cross. . . . All fancied sanctification which does not arise wholly from the blood of the cross is nothing better than Pharisaism. . . . If we would be holy, we must get to the cross, and dwell there; else, notwithstanding all our labor and diligence, and fasting, and praying, and good works, we shall be yet void of real sanctification, destitute of those humble, gracious tempers which accompany a clear view of the cross."

The one spell that can really transform us is *the cross*. The one potent watchword is, "I, if I be lifted up, will draw all men unto me" (John 12:32). The one physician for all our maladies is he who died for us, and the one remedy which he applies is the blood that cleanses from all sin. The one arm of power that can draw us out of the horrible pit and the miry clay is "the Spirit of holiness."

"For their sakes I sanctify myself, that they also might be sanctified through the truth" (John 17:19). Christ presents himself to God as the Holy One and the Consecrated One that his people may partake of his sanctification and be like himself: saints, consecrated ones, men set apart for God by the sprinkling of the blood. Through the truth they are sanctified by the power of the Holy Ghost.

"By one offering he has perfected forever them that are sanctified" (Hebrews 10:14) so that the perfection of his saints, both as to the conscience and as to personal holiness, is connected with the one offering and springs out of the one work finished upon Calvary. "By the which will we are sanctified, through the offering of the body of Jesus Christ once for all" (Hebrews 10:10). Here again the sanctification is connected with the offering of the body of Christ. Whatever place "the power of his resurrection" may hold in our spiritual history, it is the cross that is the source of all that varied fulness by which we are justified and purified. The secret of a believer's holy walk is his continual recurrence to the blood of the Surety and his daily intercourse with a crucified and risen Lord.

Nowhere does Scripture, either in its statements of doctrine or lives of the saints, teach us that here we get beyond our need of the blood or may safely cast off the divine raiment that covers our deformity. Even should we say at any time, "I am free from sin," this would be no proof of our being really holy; for the heart is deceitful above all things, and there may be ten thousand sins lurking in us, seen by God, though unseen by ourselves. "I know nothing of myself," says the apostle; *i.e.* I am not *conscious* of any failure. "But," he adds,"I am not hereby justified"; that is, my own consciousness is no proof of my sinlessness; for "he that judges me is the Lord," and the Lord may condemn me in many things in which I do not condemn myself.

Let me say to one who thinks he has reached sinlessness, "My friend, are you *sure* that you are perfectly holy? For nothing but *absolute certainty* should lead you to make so bold an affirmation regarding your freedom from all sin. Are you *sure* that you love the Lord your God with all your heart and soul? For unless you are *absolutely sure* of this, you have no right to say, I am perfectly holy; and it will be a perilous thing for you to affirm, I have no longer any need of the blood, and I refuse to go to the fountain for cleansing, seeing my going thither would be mockery. For the cross and the blood and the fountain are for the imperfect, not for the perfect; for the unrighteous, not for the righteous; and if your self-consciousness is correct, you are no longer among the imperfect or the unrighteous.

My friend, do you never sin in thought, or in word, or in desire, or in deed? Have you never a wandering thought? Is your heart as warm and are your affections as heavenly as you could possibly desire them to be? What! not one stray thought from morn to night, from night to morn? Not one wrong word, nor look, nor tone? What! no coldness, no want of fervor, no flagging of zeal, no momentary indulgence of self and sloth? What! no error (for error is *sin*), no false judgment, no failure of temper, no improper step, no imperfect plan, nothing to regret, nothing to wish unsaid or undone in the midst of a world like ours with all its provocations, its crosses, its worries, its oppositions, its heated atmosphere of infectious evil?

And are you *sure*, quite sure, that all this is the case; that your conscience is so perfectly alive, so divinely sensitive, that the faintest expressions of evil in the remotest corner of your heart would be detected? If so, you are an extraordinary man and far above him who was less than the least of all saints. You are far above him who said, "The good that I would, that I do not; and the evil that I would not, that I do." You are one whose history will require to be written by some immortal pen, as that of the man who, after a few years' believing, ceased to require any application to the cross or to be indebted to the blood for cleansing, who could look at altar and laver and mercy seat as one who had no longer any interest in their provisions; as one to whom a crucified Christ was a thing of the past, of whom he had now no need as a sin bearer or high priest or advocate or intercessor, but only as a companion and friend.

God's processes are not always rapid. His greatest works rise slowly. Swiftness of growth has been one of man's tests of greatness; not so is it with God. His trees grow slowly; the stateliest are the slowest. His creatures grow slowly, year by year; man, the noblest, grows the most slowly of all. God can afford to take his time. Man cannot. He is hasty and impatient. He will have everything to be like Jonah's gourd or like one of those fabled oriental palaces which magicians are said to call up by a word or a stamp out of the sand. He forgets how slowly the palm tree and the cedar grow. They neither spring up in a night nor perish in a night. He forgets the history of the temple: "Forty and six years was this temple in building." He insists that, because it is God's purpose that his saints should be holy, therefore they ought to be holy at once.

It is true that our standard is, and must be, perfection. For our model is the Perfect One. But the question is, Has God in Scripture anywhere led us to expect the rapidity of growth, the quick development of perfection in which some glory and because of the confessed lack of which in others they look down on these others as babes or loiterers?

Is there in Scripture any instance of a *perfect* man, excepting him who was always and absolutely without sin?

If Christians were perfect, where is the warfare, and the adversary, and the sword, and the shield? Are angels exposed to this warfare when they visit Earth? Or is it not our imperfection that in great measure produces this? And are we anywhere in Scripture led to believe that we are delivered from "the body of this death," from the battle of flesh and spirit, from the wrestling with principalities and powers, till death sets us free or our Lord shall come?

Yet we are called with a holy calling (2 Timothy 1:9) and, as so called, are bound to take the highest standard for our model of life. The slowness or swiftness of the progress does not alter the standard, nor affect our aiming at conformity to it.

This progress, rapid or gradual, springs from the forgiveness we have received and the new life imparted by the Holy Spirit. Our life is to be fruit bearing; the fruitfulness coming from our ascertained acceptance, our being "rooted and grounded in love." We taste and see that the Lord is good; that in his favor is life; that the joy of the Lord is our strength; and so we move on and up, rising from one level to another. "We know and believe the love that God has to us," and we find in this the source of goodness no less than of gladness and liberty.

The life of the justified should be a peaceful one. Being justified by faith, we have peace with God—the God of peace and the God of all grace. The world's storms have not been stilled, nor our way smoothed, nor our skies brightened, nor our enemies swept away; but the peace of God has come in and taken possession of the soul. We are cheered and comforted. God is for us, and who can be against us? The name of the Lord is our strong tower; we run into it and are safe. No evil can happen to us; no weapon that is formed against us can prosper.

The life of the justified should be a holy one, all the more because of the extent of previous unholiness. "And such were some of you: But you are washed, but you are sanctified, but you are justified in the name of the Lord Jesus, and by the Spirit of our God" (1 Corinthians 6:11). All that these marvelous and mysterious words "holy" and "holiness" imply is to be found in the life of one who has been "much forgiven." There is no spring of holiness so powerful as that which our Lord assumes: "Neither do I condemn you: Go, and sin no more" (John 8:11). Free and warm reception into the divine favor is the strongest of all motives in leading a man to seek conformity to him who has thus freely forgiven him all trespasses. A cold admission into the paternal house by the father might have repelled the prodigal and sent him back to his lusts; but the fervent kiss, the dear embrace, the best robe, the ring, the shoes, the fatted calf, the festal song—all without one moment's suspense or delay, as well as without one upbraiding word—could not but awaken shame for the past and true-hearted resolution to walk worthy of such a father and of such a generous pardon. "Revellings, banquetings, and abominable idolatries," come to be the abhorrence of him around whom the holy arms of renewed fatherhood have been so lovingly thrown. Sensuality, luxury, and the gaieties of the flesh have lost their relish to one who has tasted the fruit of the tree of life.

The life of the justified should be a loving one. It is love that has made him what he is, and shall he not love in return? Shall he not love him that begat and him also that is begotten of him? The deep true spring of love is thus revealed to us by the Lord himself: "A certain creditor had two debtors; the one owed five hundred pence, the other fifty. And when they had nothing to pay, *he frankly forgave them both.* Tell me therefore, which of them will *love* him most?" (Luke 7:41–42). Thus love produces love. The life of one on whom the fulness of the free love of God is ever shining must be a life of love. Suspense, doubt, terror, darkness must straiten and freeze; but the certainty of free and immediate love dissolves the ice, and kindles the coldest spirit into the warmth of love. "We love him because he first loved us." Love to God, love to the brethren, love to the world, spring up within us as the heavenly love flows in. Malevolence, anger, envy, jealousy, receive their death blow. The nails of the cross have gone through all these, and their deadly wound cannot be healed. They that are Christ's have crucified the flesh with its affections and lusts. Sternness, coldness, distance, depart. They are succeeded by gentleness, mildness, guilelessness, meekness, ardor, long-suffering. The tempers of the old man quit us, we know not how; in their place comes the

> charity which suffers long, and is kind, which envies not, which vaunts not itself, which is not puffed up, which does not behave itself unseemly, which seeks not her own, which is not easily provoked, which thinks no evil, which rejoices not in iniquity, but rejoices in the truth, which bears all things, which believes all things, which never fails (1 Corinthians 13:4–8).

Gentle and loving and simple should be the life of the justified; meek and lowly should they be who have been loved with such a love.

The life of the justified should be an earnest one, for everything connected with his acceptance has been earnest on the part of God; and the free forgiveness on which he has entered in believing nerves and cheers and animates. It is a spring of courage and hardihood and perseverance. It makes the coward brave. It says to the weak, Be strong! to the indolent, Arise! making the forgiving man ready to face danger and toil and loss; arming him with a new-found energy and crowning him with sure success. "Ready to spend and to be spent" is his motto now. "I am debtor" is his watchword—debtor first of all to him who forgave me, and after that, to the Church of God, redeemed with the same blood, and filled with the same Spirit; and then after that to the world around, still sunk in sin and struggling with a thousand sorrows under which it has no comforter and of whose termination it has no hope. How thoroughly in earnest should be the life of one thus pardoned—pardoned so freely, yet at such a cost to him who "gave his life a ransom for many!"

The life of the justified should be a generous one. All connected with his justification has been boundless generosity on the part of

God. He spared not his own Son, and will he not with him also freely give us all things? The love of God has been of the largest, freest kind; shall this not make us generous? The gifts of God have been all of them on the most unlimited scale; shall not this boundless liberality make us liberal in the highest and truest sense? Can a justified man be covetous or slow to part with his gold? God has given his Son; he has given his Spirit; he has given us eternal life; he has given us an everlasting kingdom. And shall these gifts not tell upon us? Shall they not expand and elevate us? Or shall they leave us narrow and shriveled as before? Surely we are called to a noble life; a life far above the common walk of humanity; a life far above that of those who, disbelieving the liberality of God, are trying to merit his favor or to purchase his kingdom by moral goodnesses or ceremonial performances of their own. Not unselfish merely, but self-denying men, we are called to be; not self pleasers, nor man pleasers, nor flesh pleasers, nor world pleasers; but pleasers of God, like Enoch (Hebrews 11:5) or like a greater than Enoch—as it is written, "Even Christ pleased not himself" (Romans 15:3). "We then that are strong ought to bear the infirmities of the weak, and *not to please ourselves;* let every one of us please his neighbor for his good to edification," that is, to the edification or building up of the body of Christ (Romans 15:2).

Selfishness, self-love, self-seeking have been in all ages the scandal of the Church of God. "All seek their own, not the things that are Jesus Christ's" (Philippians 2:21) was the sad testimony of the apostle to the Philippian church even in early days, so little had God's marvelous love told even upon those who believed it, so obstinate was the contraction of the human heart and so unwilling to yield to the enlarging pressure of an influence which men in common things deem irresistible. To love warmly, to give largely, to sympathize sincerely, to help unselfishly—these are some of the noble fruits to be expected from the belief of a love that passes knowledge. Self-sacrifice ought not to seem much to those for whom Christ has died and whom he now represents upon the throne. Generous deeds and gifts and words ought to be as natural as they are becoming in those who have been so freely loved, so abundantly pardoned, and so eternally blest. Narrow hearts are the fruits of a narrow pardon and of an uncertain favor; poor gifts are the produce of stinted and grudging giving; but large-heartedness and openhandedness may surely be looked for from those whom the boundless liberality of God has made partakers of the unsearchable riches of Christ and heirs of the kingdom which cannot be moved.

The life of the justified should be a lofty one. Littleness and meanness and earthliness do not become the pardoned. They must mount up on wings as eagles, setting their affection on things above. Having died with Christ and risen with him, they sit with him in heavenly places (Ephesians 2:6). In the world, and yet not of it, they rise above it; possessed of a heavenly citizenship (Philippians 3:20) and expecting an unearthly recompense at the return of him who has gone to prepare a place for them. High thoughts, high aims, high longings become them of whom Christ was not merely the substitute upon the cross, but the representative upon the throne—the forerunner who has entered within the veil and ever lives to intercede for us. Shall he who has been freely justified grovel in the dust, or creep along the polluted soil of earth? Shall such a justification as he has received not be the source of superhuman elevation of character, making him unworldly in his hopes, in his tastes, in his works, in the discharge of his daily calling? Shall not such a justification act upon his whole being and pervade his life; making him a thoroughly consistent man in all things; each part of his course becoming his name and prospects; his whole man symmetrical, his whole Christianity harmonious?

The life of the justified is a decided one. It does not oscillate between goodness and evil, between Christ and the world. The justifying cross has come between him and all evil things; and that which released him from the burden of guilt has, in so doing, broken the bondage of sin. Even if at any time he feels as if he could return to that country from which he set out, the cross stands in front and arrests his backward step. Between him and Egypt rolls the Red Sea, flowing in its strength so that he cannot pass. At the door of the theater or the ballroom or the revel hall stands the cross. It forbids his entrance. The world is crucified to him, and he unto the world, by the saving cross. His first look to the cross committed him. He began, and he cannot go back. It would be mean as well as perilous to do so. There is henceforth to be no mistake about him. His heart is no longer divided, and his eye no longer roams. He has taken up his cross, and he is following the Lamb. He has gone in at the strait gate and is walking along the narrow way; at the entrance thereof stands the cross barring his return. Over his entrance there was joy in Heaven; shall he at any time turn that joy into sorrow by even seeming to go back?

The life of the justified is a useful one. He has become a witness for him who has thrown over him the shadow of his cross. He can tell what the bitterness of sin is and what is the burden of guilt. He can speak of the rolling away of the stone from the sepulchre of his once dead soul and of the angel sitting on that stone clothed in light. He can make known the righteousness which he has found, and in finding which he has been brought into liberty and gladness. Out of the abundance of his heart and in the fulness of his liberated spirit, his mouth speaks. He cannot but speak of the things which he now possesses that he may induce others to come and share the fulness. He is bent on doing good. He has no hours to throw away. He knows that the time is short, and he resolves to redeem it. He will not waste a life that has been redeemed at such a cost. It is not his own, and he must keep in mind the daily responsibilities of a life thus bought for another. As one of the world's lights, in the absence of the true light, he must be always shining to lessen in some degree the darkness of Earth and to kindle heavenly light in souls who are now excluding it. As one of the sowers of the heavenly seed, he must never be idle, but watching opportunities—making opportunities for sowing it as he goes out and in; it may be in weakness; it may be in tears.

The life of the justified is the life of wisdom and truth. He has become "wise in Christ." "Christ has been made unto him wisdom" as well as righteousness. It is thus that he has become "wise unto salvation," and he feels that he must hold fast the truth that saves. To trifle with that truth, to tamper with error, would be to deny the cross. He by whom he is justified is himself *the truth,* and every man who receives that truth becomes a witness for it. By *the truth* he is saved; by *the truth* he is made free; by *the truth* he is made clean; by *the truth* he is sanctified. Therefore it is precious to him in every jot and tittle. Each fragment broken off is so much lost to his spiritual well-being, and each new discovery made in the rich field of truth is so much eternal gain. He has bought the Earth, and he will not sell it. It is his life; it is his heritage; it is his kingdom. He counts all truth precious and all error hateful. He dreads the unbelief that is undermining the foundations of truth and turning its spacious palaces into a chaos of human speculations. He calls no truth obsolete or out of date, for he knows that the truths on which he rests for eternity are the oldest of the old and yet the surest of the sure. To introduce doubts as to the one sacrifice on which he builds is to shake the cross of Calvary. To lay another foundation than that already laid is to destroy his one hope. To take the sacrificial element out of the blood is to make peace with God impossible because he is unrighteous. To substitute the church for Christ, or the priest for the herald of pardon, or the rite for the precious blood, or the sacrament for the living Christ upon the throne, or the teachings of the church for the enlightenment of the Holy Ghost—this is to turn light into darkness and then to call that darkness light. Thus taught by that Spirit who has led him to the cross, the justified man knows how to discern truth from error. He has the unction from the Holy One and knows all things (1 John 2:20); he has the anointing which is truth and is no lie (1 John 2:27); and he can try the spirits, whether they are of God (1 John 4:1).

Want of sensitiveness to the difference between truth and error is one of the evil features of modern Protestantism. Sounding words, well-executed pictures, and pretentious logic carry away multitudes. The distinction between Gospel and no Gospel is very decided and very momentous; yet many will come away from a sermon in which the free Gospel has been overlaid and not be sensible of the lack, praising the preacher. The conversions of recent years have not the depth of other days. Consciences are half-awakened and half-pacified; the wound is slightly laid open, and slightly healed—hence the want of spiritual discernment as to truth and error. The conscience is not sensitive, else it would at once refuse and resent any statement, however well argued or painted, which encroached in the slightest degree upon the free Gospel of God's love in Christ; which interposed any obstacle between the sinner and the cross; or which merely declaimed about the cross without telling us especially how it saves and how it purifies. We need *sensitive* but not *morbid* consciences to keep us stedfast in the faith and to preserve our spiritual eyesight unimpaired, remembering the apostle's words, "He that lacks these things is *blind, and cannot see afar off,* and has forgotten that he was purged from his old sins" (2 Peter 1:9). Censoriousness is one thing, and spiritual discernment is quite another. To avoid the first we do not need to give up the second; though the "liberality" of modern times would recommend us to be charitable to error and not very tenacious of any Bible truth, seeing that nothing in an age of culture can be received but that which has been pronounced credible by philosophy or science and which the "verifying faculty" has adjudged to be true!

The life of the justified must be one of praise and prayer. His justification has drawn him near to God. It has opened his lips and enlarged his heart. He cannot but praise; he cannot but pray. He has ten thousand things to ask for; he has ten thousand things for which to give thanks. He knows what it is to speak in psalms and hymns and spiritual songs, singing with grace in his heart to the Lord (Colossians 3:16).

The life of the justified is one of watchfulness. Forgiveness has altered all his circumstances and hopes. It has brought him into a new world from which are shut out things he was formerly familiar with and into which are introduced things which he knew not. He sees and hears what he never saw nor heard before, and he ceases to see and hear what but lately he delighted in. He is no longer satisfied with things as they are. He expects changes and wishes that they were come. The present has become less to him, the future more; and in that future the one absorbing object is the reappearing of him, whom not having seen he loves.

That the future should be a mere repetition of the present—with a few scientific and political improvements—is quite enough for the worldly man. But the man who, by his new connection with the cross, has been transported into a new region is not content that it should be so. He wants a better future and a more congenial world; he desires a state of things in which the new object of his love shall be all. And learning from Scripture that such a new condition of things is to be expected, and that of that new state Christ is himself to be the first and last, he looks eagerly out for the fulfilment of these hopes. Learning, moreover, that the arrival of this King and his kingdom is to be sudden, he is led to wait and watch—all the more because everything here, in the world's daily history of change and noise and revelry is fitted to throw him off his guard. His justification does not lull him asleep. His faith does not make him heedless of the future. It is the substance of things hoped for, the evidence of things not seen. It says, Let us not sleep, as do others; but let us watch and be sober: Watch, for ye know neither the day nor the hour when the Son of Man comes. Many a trial of her watchfulness has the Church had, many a disappointment has her faith sustained; but she does not despond nor give way, remembering the promise, "He that shall come will come, and will not tarry." Her faith keeps up her vigilance, and her vigilance invigorates her faith. In the darkest hour faith says, "I am my beloved's, and my beloved is mine"; and hope adds, "Make haste, my beloved, and be thou like to a roe or a young hart upon the mountains of spices."

The Church watches because of present evil and coming good, that she may be kept undefiled from the one and may attain unto the other. Danger from enemies and the prospect of speedy victory over them keep her awake. Fear of losing sight of the cross and so again walking in darkness; suspicion both of the good and the evil things of Earth—its flatteries and its menaces, its toils, its cares, its amusements, its pleasures; anxiety about keeping her garments unspotted and her conscience clean; the sight of the sleeping millions around; and the knowledge that it is upon a sleeping world that the Lord is to come—these things act powerfully as stimulants and bid her be watchful.

To be among the foolish virgins, without oil and with a dying lamp, when the midnight cry goes forth; to be near the door and yet shut out; to hear the announcement, "The marriage of the Lamb is come, and his wife has made herself ready," and yet not be ready; to be summoned to the festival and yet to be without the bridal and the festal dress; to love and then to fall from love; to draw the sword and then in faint heartedness to sheathe it; to run well for a while and then to slacken speed; to war against Satan as the prince of darkness and yield to him as an angel of light; to set out with condemning the world and then to mingle with it; to cleave like Demas to the saints and then to forsake them; to be among the twelve for a season and then to be a traitor at the last; to be lifted up like Capernaum to Heaven and then to be thrust down to Hell; to be among the sons of light and then to fall from Heaven like Lucifer, son of the morning; to sit down in the upper chamber with the Lord and then to betray the Son of Man with a kiss; to put on a goodly garment of fair profession and then to walk naked in shame—these are the solemn thoughts that crowd in upon the justified man and keep him watchful.

They who know not what it is to be "accepted in the Beloved" and to "rejoice in hope of the glory of God" may fall asleep. He dare not; he knows what he is risking and what one hour of slumber may cost him, and he must be wakeful. He does not make election his opiate and say, I am safe, I may sleep or wake as I please. He says, I am safe; but this only makes me doubly vigilant that I may not dishonor him who has saved me; and even though I may not finally fall away, I know not how much I may lose by one day's slothfulness or how much I may gain by maintaining that watchful attitude to which, as the expectant of an absent Lord, I am called. "Blessed is he that watches," and even though I could not see the reason for this, I will act upon it that I may realize the promised blessedness. He who has called me to vigilance can make me partaker of its joy. He can make my watchtower, lonely and dark as it may seem, none other than the house of God and the very gate of Heaven.

INDEX

Scripture Index

THE CRISIS OF OUR TIME

Historians have christened the thirteenth century the Age of Faith and termed the eighteenth century the Age of Reason. The twentieth century has been called many things: the Atomic Age, the Age of Inflation, the Age of the Tyrant, the Age of Aquarius. But it deserves one name more than the others: the Age of Irrationalism. Contemporary secular intellectuals are anti-intellectual. Contemporary philosophers are anti-philosophy. Contemporary theologians are anti-theology.

In past centuries secular philosophers have generally believed that knowledge is possible to man. Consequently they expended a great deal of thought and effort trying to justify knowledge. In the twentieth century, however, the optimism of the secular philosophers has all but disappeared. They despair of knowledge.

Like their secular counterparts, the great theologians and doctors of the church taught that knowledge is possible to man. Yet the theologians of the twentieth century have repudiated that belief. They also despair of knowledge. This radical skepticism has filtered down from the philosophers and theologians and penetrated our entire culture, from television to music to literature. *The Christian in the twentieth century is confronted with an overwhelming cultural consensus—sometimes stated explicitly, but most often implicitly: Man does not and cannot know anything truly.*

What does this have to do with Christianity? Simply this: If man can know nothing truly, man can truly know nothing. We cannot know that the Bible is the Word of God, that Christ died for the sins of his people, or that Christ is alive today at the right hand of the Father. Unless knowledge is possible, Christianity is nonsensical, for it claims to be knowledge. What is at stake in the twentieth century is not simply a single doctrine, such as the virgin birth, or the existence of Hell, as important as those doctrines may be, but the whole of Christianity itself. If knowledge is not possible to man, it is worse than silly to argue points of doctrine—it is insane.

The irrationalism of the present age is so thorough-going and pervasive that even the Remnant—the segment of the professing church that remains faithful—has accepted much of it, frequently

123

without even being aware of what it was accepting. In some circles this irrationalism has become synonymous with piety and humility, and those who oppose it are denounced as rationalists—as though to be logical were a sin. Our contemporary anti-theologians make a contradiction and call it a Mystery. The faithful ask for truth and are given Paradox. If any balk at swallowing the absurdities of the anti-theologians, they are frequently marked as heretics or schismatics who seek to act independently of God.

There is no greater threat facing the true church of Christ at this moment than the irrationalism that now controls our entire culture. Totalitarianism, guilty of tens of millions of murders, including those of millions of Christians, is to be feared, but not nearly so much as the idea that we do not and cannot know the truth. Hedonism, the popular philosophy of America, is not to be feared so much as the belief that logic—that "mere human logic," to use the religious irrationalists' own phrase—is futile. The attacks on truth, on revelation, on the intellect, and on logic are renewed daily. But note well: The misologists—the haters of logic—use logic to demonstrate the futility of using logic. The anti-intellectuals construct intricate intellectual arguments to prove the insufficiency of the intellect. The anti-theologians use the revealed Word of God to show that there can be no revealed Word of God—or that if there could, it would remain impenetrable darkness and Mystery to our finite minds.

Nonsense Has Come

Is it any wonder that the world is grasping at straws—the straws of experientialism, mysticism, and drugs? After all, if people are told that the Bible contains insoluble mysteries, then is not a flight into mysticism to be expected? On what grounds can it be condemned? Certainly not on logical grounds or Biblical grounds, if logic is futile and the Bible unintelligible. Moreover, if it cannot be condemned on logical or Biblical grounds, it cannot be condemned at all. If people are going to have a religion of the mysterious, they will not adopt Christianity: They will have a genuine mystery religion. "Those who call for Nonsense," C.S. Lewis once wrote, "will find that it comes." And that is precisely what has happened. The popularity of Eastern mysticism, of drugs, and of religious experience is the logical consequence of the irrationalism of the twentieth century. There can and will be no new Reformation—and no reconstruction of society—unless and until the irrationalism of the age is totally repudiated by Christians.

The Church Defenseless

Yet how shall they do it? The spokesmen for Christianity have been fatally infected with irrationalism. The seminaries, which annually train thousands of men to teach millions of Christians, are the finishing schools of irrationalism, completing the job begun by the government schools and colleges. Some of the pulpits of the most conservative churches (we are not speaking of the apostate churches) are occupied by graduates of the anti-theological schools. These products of modern anti-theological education, when asked to give a reason for the hope that is in them, can generally respond with only the intellectual analogue of a shrug—a mumble about Mystery. They have not grasped—and therefore cannot teach those for whom they are responsible—the first truth: "And ye shall know the truth." Many, in fact, explicitly deny it, saying that, at best, we possess only "pointers" to the truth, or something "similar" to the truth, a mere analogy. Is the impotence of the Christian church a puzzle? Is the fascination with pentecostalism and faith healing among members of conservative churches an enigma? Not when one understands the sort of studied nonsense that is purveyed in the name of God in the seminaries.

The Trinity Foundation

The creators of The Trinity Foundation firmly believe that theology is too important to be left to the licensed theologians—the graduates of the schools of theology. They have created The Trinity Foundation for the express purpose of teaching the faithful all that the Scriptures contain—not warmed over, baptized, secular philosophies. Each member of the board of directors of The Trinity Foundation has signed this oath: "I believe that the Bible alone and the Bible in its entirety is the Word of God and, therefore, inerrant in the autographs. I believe that the system of truth presented in the Bible is best summarized in the Westminster Confession of Faith. So help me God."

The ministry of The Trinity Foundation is the presentation of the system of truth taught in Scripture as clearly and as completely as possible. We do not regard obscurity as a virtue, nor confusion as a sign of spirituality. Confusion, like all error, is sin, and teaching that confusion is all that Christians can hope for is doubly sin.

The presentation of the truth of Scripture necessarily involves the rejection of error. The Foundation has exposed and will continue to expose the irrationalism of the twentieth century, whether its current spokesman be an existentialist philosopher or a professed Reformed theologian. We oppose anti-intellectualism, whether it be espoused by a neo-orthodox theologian or a fundamentalist evangelist. We reject misology, whether it be on the lips of a neo-evangelical or those of a Roman Catholic charismatic. To each error we bring the brilliant light of Scripture, proving all things, and holding fast to that which is true.

The Primacy of Theory

The ministry of The Trinity Foundation is not a "practical" ministry. If you are a pastor, we will not enlighten you on how to organize an ecumenical prayer meeting in your community or how to double church attendance in a year. If you are a homemaker, you will have to read elsewhere to find out how to become a total woman. If you are a businessman, we will not tell you how to develop a social conscience. The professing church is drowning in such "practical" advice.

The Trinity Foundation is unapologetically theoretical in its outlook, believing that theory without practice is dead, and that practice without theory is blind. The trouble with the professing church is not primarily in its practice, but in its theory. Christians do not know, and many do not even care to know, the doctrines of Scripture. Doctrine is intellectual, and Christians are generally anti-intellectual. Doctrine is ivory tower philosophy, and they scorn ivory towers. The ivory tower, however, is the control tower of a civilization. It is a fundamental, theoretical mistake of the practical men to think that they can be merely practical, for practice is always the practice of some theory. The relationship between theory and practice is the relationship between cause and effect. If a person believes correct theory, his practice will tend to be correct. The practice of contemporary Christians is immoral because it is the practice of false theories. It is a major theoretical mistake of the practical men to think that they can ignore the ivory towers of the philosophers and theologians as irrelevant to their lives. Every action that the "practical" men take is governed by the thinking that has occurred in some ivory tower—whether that tower be the British Museum, the Academy, a home in Basel, Switzerland, or a tent in Israel.

In Understanding Be Men

It is the first duty of the Christian to understand correct theory—correct doctrine—and thereby implement correct practice. This order—first theory, then practice—is both logical and Biblical. It is, for example, exhibited in Paul's epistle to the Romans, in which he spends the first eleven chapters expounding theory and the last five discussing practice. The contemporary teachers of Christians have not only reversed the order, they have inverted the Pauline emphasis on theory and practice. The virtually complete failure of the teachers of the professing church to instruct the faithful in correct doctrine is the cause of the misconduct and cultural impotence of Christians. The church's lack of power is the result of its lack of truth. The *Gospel* is the power of God, not religious experience or personal relationship. The church has no power because it has abandoned the Gospel, the good news, for a religion of experientialism. Twentieth century American Christians are children carried about by every wind of doctrine, not knowing what they believe, or even if they believe anything for certain.

The chief purpose of The Trinity Foundation is to counteract the irrationalism of the age and to expose the errors of the teachers of the church. Our emphasis—on the Bible as the sole source of truth, on the primacy of the intellect, on the supreme importance of correct doctrine, and on the necessity for systematic and logical thinking—is almost unique in Christendom. To the extent that the church survives—and she will survive and flourish—it will be because of her increasing acceptance of these basic ideas and their logical implications.

We believe that The Trinity Foundation is filling a vacuum in Christendom. We are saying that Christianity is intellectually defensible—that, in fact, it is the only intellectually defensible system of thought. We are saying that God has made the wisdom of this world—whether that wisdom be called science, religion, philosophy, or common sense—foolishness. We are appealing to all Christians who have not conceded defeat in the intellectual battle with the world to join us in our efforts to raise a standard to which all men of sound mind can repair.

The love of truth, of God's Word, has all but disappeared in our time. We are committed to and pray for a great instauration. But though we may not see this reformation of Christendom in our lifetimes, we believe it is our duty to present the whole counsel of God because Christ has commanded it. The results of our teaching are in God's hands, not ours. Whatever those results, his Word is never taught in vain, but always accomplishes the result that he intended it to accomplish. Professor Gordon H. Clark has stated our view well:

> There have been times in the history of God's people, for example, in the days of Jeremiah, when refreshing grace and widespread revival were not to be expected: The time was one of chastisement. If this twentieth century is of a similar nature, individual Christians here and there can find comfort and strength in a study of God's Word. But if God has decreed happier days for us and if we may expect a world-shaking and genuine spiritual awakening, then it is the author's belief that a zeal for souls, however necessary, is not the sufficient condition. Have there not been devout saints in every age, numerous enough to carry on a revival? Twelve such persons are plenty. What distinguishes the arid ages from the period of the Reformation, when nations were moved as they had not been since Paul preached in Ephesus, Corinth, and Rome, is the latter's fullness of knowledge of God's Word. To echo an early Reformation thought, when the ploughman and the garage attendant know the Bible as well as the theologian does, and know it better than some contemporary theologians, then the desired awakening shall have already occurred.

In addition to publishing books, the Foundation publishes a monthly newsletter, *The Trinity Review*. Subscriptions to *The Review* are free; please write to the address below to become a subscriber. If you would like further information or would like to join us in our work, please let us know.

The Trinity Foundation is a non-profit foundation tax-exempt under section 501(c)(3) of the Internal Revenue Code of 1954. You can help us disseminate the Word of God through your tax-deductible contributions to the Foundation.

And we know that the Son of God has come, and has given us an understanding, that we may know him that is true, and we are in him that is true, in his Son Jesus Christ. This is the true God, and eternal life.

John W. Robbins

INTELLECTUAL AMMUNITION

The Trinity Foundation is committed to the reconstruction of philosophy and theology along Biblical lines. We regard God's command to bring all our thoughts into conformity with Christ very seriously, and the books listed below are designed to accomplish that goal. They are written with two subordinate purposes: (1) to demolish all secular claims to knowledge; and (2) to build a system of truth based upon the Bible alone.

Philosophy

Behaviorism and Christianity, Gordon H. Clark $6.95
Behaviorism *is a critique of both secular and religious behaviorists. It includes chapters on John Watson, Edgar S. Singer Jr., Gilbert Ryle, B.F. Skinner, and Donald MacKay. Clark's refutation of behaviorism and his argument for a Christian doctrine of man are unanswerable.*

A Christian Philosophy of Education $8.95
Gordon H. Clark
The first edition of this book was published in 1946. It sparked the contemporary interest in Christian schools. Dr. Clark thoroughly revised and updated it, and it is needed now more than ever. Its chapters include: The Need for a World-View, The Christian World-View, The Alternative to Christian Theism, Neutrality, Ethics, The Christian Philosophy of Education, Academic Matters, Kindergarten to University. Three appendices are included as well: The Relationship of Public Education to Christianity, A Protestant World-View, and Art and the Gospel.

A Christian View of Men and Things $10.95
Gordon H. Clark
No other book achieves what A Christian View *does: the presentation of Christianity as it applies to history, politics, ethics, science, religion, and epistemology. Clark's command of both*

worldly philosophy and Scripture is evident on every page, and the result is a breathtaking and invigorating challenge to the wisdom of this world.

Clark Speaks From The Grave, Gordon H. Clark $3.95

Dr. Clark chides some of his critics for their failure to defend Christianity competently. Clark Speaks is a stimulating and illuminating discussion of the errors of contemporary apologists.

Education, Christianity, and the State $8.95
J. Gresham Machen

Machen was one of the foremost educators, theologians, and defenders of Christianity in the twentieth century. The author of numerous scholarly books, Machen saw clearly that if Christianity is to survive and flourish, a system of Christian grade schools must be established. This collection of essays captures his thoughts on education over nearly three decades.

Essays on Ethics and Politics, Gordon H. Clark $10.95

Clark's essays, written over the course of five decades, are a major statement of Christian ethics.

Gordon H. Clark: Personal Recollections $6.95
John W. Robbins, editor

Friends of Dr. Clark have written their recollections of the man. Contributors include family members, colleagues, students, and friends such as Harold Lindsell, Carl Henry, Ronald Nash, Dwight Zeller, and Mary Crumpacker. The book includes an extensive bibliography of Clark's work.

Historiography: Secular and Religious $13.95
Gordon H. Clark

In this masterful work, Clark applies his philosophy to the writing of history, examining all the major schools of historiography.

An Introduction to Christian Philosophy $8.95
Gordon H. Clark

In 1966 Clark delivered three lectures on philosophy at Whea-

ton College. In these lectures he criticizes secular philosophy and launches a philosophical revolution in the name of Christ.

Language and Theology, Gordon H. Clark $9.95
There are two main currents in twentieth-century philosophy— language philosophy and existentialism. Both are hostile to Christianity. Clark disposes of language philosophy in this brilliant critique of Bertrand Russell, Ludwig Wittgenstein, Rudolf Carnap, A.J. Ayer, Langdon Gilkey, and many others.

Logic, Gordon H. Clark $8.95
Written as a textbook for Christian schools, Logic *is another unique book from Clark's pen. His presentation of the laws of thought, which must be followed if Scripture is to be understood correctly, and which are found in Scripture itself, is both clear and thorough.* Logic *is an indispensable book for the thinking Christian.*

Logic Workbook, Elihu Carranza $11.95
Designed to be used in conjunction with Clark's textbook Logic, *this* Workbook *contains hundreds of exercises and test questions on perforated pages for ease of use by students.*

Logic Workbook Answer Key, Elihu Carranza $4.95
The Key *contains answers to all the exercises and tests in the* Workbook.

Lord God of Truth, Concerning the Teacher $7.95
Gordon H. Clark and Aurelius Augustine
This essay by Clark summarizes many of the most telling arguments against empiricism and defends the Biblical teaching that we know God and truth immediately. The dialogue by Augustine is a refutation of empirical language philosophy.

The Philosophy of Science and Belief in God $7.95
Gordon H. Clark
In opposing the contemporary idolatry of science, Clark analyzes three major aspects of science: the problem of motion, Newtonian science, and modern theories of physics. His conclusion is that science, while it may be useful, is always false; and he demonstrates

its falsity in numerous ways. Since science is always false, it can offer no objection to the Bible and Christianity.

Religion, Reason and Revelation, Gordon H. Clark $9.95
One of Clark's apologetical masterpieces, Religion, Reason and Revelation *has been praised for the clarity of its thought and language. It includes chapters on Is Christianity a Religion?, Faith and Reason, Inspiration and Language, Revelation and Morality, and God and Evil. It is must reading for all serious Christians.*

Thales to Dewey: A History of Philosophy   paper $11.95
Gordon H. Clark   hardback $16.95
This is the best one volume history of philosophy in English.

Three Types of Religious Philosophy $6.95
Gordon H. Clark
In this book on apologetics, Clark examines empiricism, rationalism, dogmatism, and contemporary irrationalism, which does not rise to the level of philosophy. He offers a solution to the question, "How can Christianity be defended before the world?"

William James and John Dewey $8.95
Gordon H. Clark
William James and John Dewey are two of the most influential philosophers America has produced. Their philosophies of instrumentalism and pragmatism are hostile to Christianity, and Clark demolishes their arguments completely.

Theology

The Atonement, Gordon H. Clark $8.95
This is a major section of Clark's multi-volume systematic theology. In The Atonement, *Clark discusses the covenants, the virgin birth and incarnation, federal headship and representation, the relationship between God's sovereignty and justice, and much more. He analyzes traditional views of the atonement and criticizes them in the light of Scripture alone.*

The Biblical Doctrine of Man, Gordon H. Clark $6.95
Is man soul and body or soul, spirit, and body? What is the image of God? Is Adam's sin imputed to his children? Is evolution true? Are men totally depraved? What is the heart? These are some of the questions discussed and answered from Scripture in this book.

Cornelius Van Til: The Man and The Myth $2.45
John W. Robbins
The actual teachings of this eminent Philadelphia theologian have been obscured by the myths that surround him. This book penetrates those myths and criticizes Van Til's surprisingly unorthodox views of God and the Bible.

The Everlasting Righteousness, Horatius Bonar $8.95
Originally published in 1874, the language of Bonar's masterpiece on justification by faith alone has been updated and Americanized for easy reading and clear understanding. This is one of the best books ever written on justification.

Faith and Saving Faith, Gordon H. Clark $6.95
The views of the Roman Catholic church, John Calvin, Thomas Manton, John Owen, Charles Hodge, and B.B. Warfield are discussed in this book. Is the object of faith a person or a proposition? Is faith more than belief? Is belief more than thinking with assent, as Augustine said? In a world chaotic with differing views of faith, Clark clearly explains the Biblical view of faith and saving faith.

God's Hammer: The Bible and Its Critics $8.95
Gordon H. Clark
The starting point of Christianity, the doctrine on which all other doctrines depend, is "The Bible alone is the Word of God written, and therefore inerrant in the autographs." Over the centuries the opponents of Christianity, with Satanic shrewdness, have concentrated their attacks on the truthfulness and completeness of the Bible. In the twentieth century the attack is not so much in the fields of history and archaeology as in philosophy. Clark's brilliant defense of the complete truthfulness of the Bible is captured in this collection of eleven major essays.

Guide to the Westminster Confession and Catechism $13.95
James E. Bordwine
This large book contains the full text of both the Westminster Confession (both original and American versions) and the Larger Catechism. In addition, it offers a chapter-by-chapter summary of the Confession and a unique index to both the Confession and the Catechism.

The Holy Spirit, Gordon H. Clark $8.95
This discussion of the third person of the Trinity is both concise and exact. Clark includes chapters on the work of the Spirit, santification, and Pentecostalism. This book is part of his multi-volume systematic theology that began appearing in print in 1985.

The Incarnation, Gordon H. Clark $8.95
Who is Christ? The attack on the incarnation in the nineteenth and twentieth centuries has been vigorous, but the orthodox response has been lame. Clark reconstructs the doctrine of the incarnation, building and improving upon the Chalcedonian definition.

In Defense of Theology, Gordon H. Clark $9.95
There are four groups to whom Clark addresses this book: average Christians who are uninterested in theology, atheists and agnostics, religious experientialists, and serious Christians. The vindication of the knowledge of God against the objections of three of these groups is the first step in theology.

The Johannine Logos, Gordon H. Clark $5.95
Clark analyzes the relationship between Christ, who is the truth, and the Bible. He explains why John used the same word to refer to both Christ and his teaching. Chapters deal with the Prologue to John's Gospel, Logos and Rheemata, Truth, and Saving Faith.

Justification by Faith Alone, Charles Hodge $8.95
Charles Hodge of Princeton Seminary was the best American theologian of the nineteenth century. Here in one volume are his two major essays on justification. This book is essential in defending the faith.

Predestination, Gordon H. Clark $8.95

Clark thoroughly discusses one of the most controversial and pervasive doctrines of the Bible: that God is, quite literally, Almighty. Free will, the origin of evil, God's omniscience, creation, and the new birth are all presented within a Scriptural framework. The objections of those who do not believe in the Almighty God are considered and refuted. This edition also contains the text of the booklet, Predestination in the Old Testament.

Sanctification, Gordon H. Clark $8.95

In this book, which is part of Clark's multi-volume systematic theology, he discusses historical theories of sanctification, the sacraments, and the Biblical doctrine of sanctification.

Scripture Twisting in the Seminaries
Part 1: Feminism, John W. Robbins $5.95

An analysis of the views of three graduates of Westminster Seminary on the role of women in the church.

Today's Evangelism: Counterfeit or Genuine? $6.95
Gordon H. Clark

Clark compares the methods and messages of today's evangelists with Scripture, and finds that Christianity is on the wane because the Gospel has been distorted or lost. This is an extremely useful and enlightening book.

The Trinity, Gordon H. Clark $8.95

Apart from the doctrine of Scripture, no teaching of the Bible is more important than the doctrine of God. Clark's defense of the orthodox doctrine of the Trinity is a principal portion of Clark's systematic theology. There are chapters on the deity of Christ, Augustine, the incomprehensibility of God, Bavinck and Van Til, and the Holy Spirit, among others.

What Calvin Says, W. Gary Crampton $7.95

This is both a readable and thorough introduction to the theology of John Calvin.

What Do Presbyterians Believe? Gordon H. Clark $8.95
This classic introduction to Christian doctrine has been republished. It is the best commentary on the Westminster Confession of Faith that has ever been written.

Commentaries on the New Testament

Colossians, Gordon H. Clark $6.95
Ephesians, Gordon H. Clark $8.95
First Corinthians, Gordon H. Clark $10.95
First John, Gordon H. Clark $10.95
First and Second Thessalonians, Gordon H. Clark $5.95
New Heavens, New Earth (First and Second Peter) $10.95
    Gordon H. Clark
The Pastoral Epistles (I and II Timothy and Titus) $9.95
    Gordon H. Clark
All of Clark's commentaries are expository, not technical, and are written for the Christian layman. His purpose is to explain the text clearly and accurately so that the Word of God will be thoroughly known by every Christian.

The Trinity Library

We will send you one copy of each of the 45 books listed above for $250. You may also order the books you want individually on the order blank on the next page. Because some of the books are in short supply, we must reserve the right to substitute others of equal or greater value in The Trinity Library. This special offer expires June 30, 1997.

ORDER FORM

Name   _____

Address   _____

_____

Please: ☐ add my name to the mailing list for *The Trinity Review*.
I understand that there is no charge for the *Review* in the
United States. (Ten dollars per year to foreign ad-
dresses.)

       ☐ accept my tax deductible contribution of $_____ for
the work of the Foundation.

       ☐ send me _____ copies of *The Everlasting Righ-
teousness*. I enclose as payment $_____.

       ☐ send me the Trinity Library of 45 books.
I enclose $250 as full payment.

       ☐ send me the following books. I enclose full payment in
the amount of $_____ for them.

_____

_____

_____

_____

_____

_____

Mail to: The Trinity Foundation
Post Office Box 1666
Hobbs, NM 88240